FOUNT CHILDREN'S BIBLE

Andrew Knowles

illustrated by
Bert Bouman

The text of the Fount Children's Bible is based on an
original Dutch text by Karel Eykman.

First published in two volumes as "Woord voor Woord"
by Zomer & Keuning, Wageningen, Netherlands in 1976.

© 1976 Zomer & Keuning Boeken B.V., Wageningen

First published in English by Fount Paperbacks, London, 1981

English translation © William Collins Sons & Co Ltd, Glasgow, 1981

ISBN 0 00 625894 8

Co-edition arranged with the
help of Angus Hudson Limited

Made and printed in Great Britain by
Purnell & Sons Ltd. (Bristol) and London

Before We Begin . . .

In the Bible, we find the stories of many people, old and young, rich and poor, who shared their lives with God. Men and women who were changed by being caught up in the great adventure of loving God and serving Him in the world He has made. Some of them had very hard lives, and made many mistakes. But at the end of the day they could all say that God is real, and that knowing Him is the key to life. These are the folk we'll be meeting in this book.

Abraham was the first to be called God's special friend. Although he couldn't see God, he trusted Him so firmly that he was prepared to leave his home and go in search of a new life. After Abraham came others. Each of them discovered something new about God, as well as realizing that the old lessons were still true. Eventually there rose up a whole nation, the Jewish people, who were so close to God that they were known as the Chosen Race.

God gave the Jews a land of their own and promised to bless them in many ways, if they would obey Him. But as time went by, things began to go wrong. Many Jews drifted from God's way, and started worshipping man-made idols. In the end they were defeated by another nation, and dragged away as prisoners into Exile. It was while they were away from home that they turned again to God and asked Him for help. They told each other the old stories of what God had done for them in the past. And they dared to hope that God still had a plan for them. In due course all the stories and books were collected together, and the resulting work is known as the Old Testament.

Contents

The Old Testament

In the Beginning . . .

In the beginning there was nothing, absolutely nothing. No earth or sky or sea, just darkness. Empty, shapeless gloom.

And then the Spirit of God began to move, like a great wind stirring. And God spoke in the darkness: "Let there be light!" And straight away there was light, scattering the darkness and showing up infinite space. "That's good!" said God. "From now on, when it's dark that will be 'night', and when it's light, that will be 'day'." And so it was. The evening came, the night passed and then light returned. That was one day. And after that day came another.

9

God said, "Now we need an 'above' above and a 'below' below." Very carefully He made the earth, and over it He hung a vast blue sky. He stood back. It was the best earth and the best sky that He had ever seen. "And that's good too!" said God. At that moment the sky grew dark, the twilight came, and then the night. Another day was over.

The following morning God said, "And now the earth needs tidying up. We'll put all the water in one place, and all the dry land in another." When He had finished that, God made plants to cover the land. Daisies and buttercups and dandelions appeared. All sorts of trees began to grow: oak trees, apple trees, cherry trees . . . "It's looking good", said God. Another evening came and next morning it grew light again. That was the third day.

Then God said, "The daylight needs working on, and the night is still too dark." So saying, He made the sun to light the world during the day, and the moon to light the sky during the night. Proudly, He hung them in space. He also made the stars; so many that no one could ever count them. At twilight, the first evening star appeared, then the full moon, and then a glorious network of stars. "It's all coming on well!", said God. That was the fourth day.

Next God turned His attention to the sea. "I want these waters teeming with life", He said. And it was so. In no time at all, there were millions of little fish darting in the shallows, and great monsters patrolling the deep. God made birds, too. He watched them soaring through the air, riding the wind, and calling to each other. "Now that's really something!", said God. Just then dusk fell over the water, the sky grew dark and the birds and fishes went to sleep. So ended the fifth day.

The next day God said, "Now let Me see. We have fish in the sea, birds in the air, and ah, yes – we need creatures on the land." That morning God made all the wild animals: lions and tigers and bears and crocodiles. In the afternoon He made friendlier creatures: cows and sheep and rabbits and cats. Never was there such variety – from antelopes to ants and from lizards to limpets! "I really enjoyed making them", said God. "But there's still someone missing. Someone to care for it all. Someone for me to talk to . . ."

11

And that was why God made Mankind. "Take a good look round", said God, as the first human being stood blinking at the sunset. "All that you see is yours. I want you to enjoy it and take care of it. There are fish in the sea, and birds in the air, and animals in the forest. It's up to you to find them all and give them names. You'll see plenty of fruit on the trees to keep you going until you learn to hunt. Goodnight!"

12

That was the sixth day. "I think that's everything", said God, looking it over with great delight. "Though I say it Myself, it's really very good!"

So the whole universe was completed. On the seventh day God had a nice long rest, and enjoyed looking at all He had made.

13

The First People

The Jews told this story about the very first Man:

The Lord God took some clay from the ground, and made the shape of a man. Then He breathed gently into the nostrils. The man's chest rose and fell. His eyes opened. He began to live.

The Lord gave him a Garden to live in, saying, "All this is for you. Help yourself to anything you like. But never touch the tree in the middle of the Garden. That tree gives knowledge of good and evil. The day you eat its fruit, you will die."

God had made Man to keep Him company and to look after the world. God and Man were alike in many ways. They were both creative. They were both loving. They both enjoyed a good discussion. In due course, God brought all the animals to the Man, to be given their names. "Elephant", he would say, or "Kangaroo", or "Grasshopper". It was great fun.

But God felt sorry for Man. "Not one of the animals is really like him," said God, "he needs someone to live with. Someone to share his life."

That night, God took a rib from Man's side, and made Woman. When Man awoke the following morning, he found a wife lying asleep beside him. He was overjoyed. He took her hand and her eyes opened. She smiled.

"You are my other half. The person I've been looking for to share my life", he said.

"And you are my husband", she replied.

How Things Went Wrong

The Man's name was Adam. His wife's name was Eve. They lived together in the Garden for many happy months. They played with the animals and feasted on the fruit. It was a perfect way of life. They had no clothes, but that didn't worry them for a moment.

One day, Eve was gathering blackberries for supper when she heard a voice behind her.

"Is it true that you're not supposed to come anywhere near here?" it said. It was a very smooth and silky voice, and extremely cultured. Eve turned to see a snake talking to her.

"We can go where we like and eat what we like", said Eve. "God said we were to help ourselves."

"Oh, really?" said the snake. "I must have misunderstood. Forgive me." He looked unblink-

15

ingly at Eve, and added thoughtfully, "Er – have you tried the fruit of the tree over there?" He nodded towards the tree of the knowledge of good and evil. "It's really very fine. Very fine indeed."

"No, I haven't actually", said Eve. "God warned us that the fruit of that tree would kill us."

The snake chuckled. "Oh dear, oh dear!" he murmured to himself. "The things the Almighty gets up to!" He spoke to the woman. "I hardly think it will do you any harm. After all, poison hasn't been invented yet! Now come on, have a little taste. Why not?"

So Eve plucked the fruit and tasted it. A strange feeling came over her. The feeling of having done something wrong. Hurriedly, she picked some more, and took it back to Adam. They ate the fruit for supper, and sat in gloomy silence. There didn't seem to be anything to talk about. Anyway, Eve was feeling very embarrassed, sitting there without any clothes. She tried to cover herself with leaves.

Suddenly, they heard God coming. He was calling them. "Adam! Where are you? Eve?" Without thinking, they dived into the bushes. But the Lord knew where they were.

"What's the matter, Adam?" He said when He found them.

"Nothing, Lord", said Adam. "It's just that we feel a bit embarrassed, you know, sitting here with no clothes on."

"Whatever made you think of that?" said God. "You haven't eaten from that tree have you?"

"I don't know what I've eaten", said Adam, lying for all he was worth. "That wife you gave me sees to the food. I just eat what's put in front of me."

Eve blushed. "Please Lord, it was from the tree. I met a very nice snake who said it would be all right."

God was very angry. "You've done the one thing I told you not to do," He said, "and now evil has crept into my world. Already you are shy about being naked, and blaming each other for what has happened." He looked at them. "You must leave this Garden. From now on you'll have to scratch a living from the soil. You'll need to make clothes and grow food. Nothing will come easily – not even childbirth. And one day, you will die."

And that was how things went wrong. And that was why Adam and Eve had to leave the Garden. And that was why life became hard.

The First Murder

Now Adam and Eve had to do everything for themselves. They built a hut and made a fire. They killed animals for food, and used the skins for clothes. Somehow they managed to keep themselves alive. It wasn't long before Eve gave birth to a baby boy. She called him Cain. Later, she had another, and called him Abel. They were very different from each other. Cain became a farmer, and Abel became a shepherd. To tell you the truth, they didn't always see eye to eye. Like the occasion when Abel's goat ate all Cain's cabbages!

One day, both Cain and Abel offered sacrifices to God. Cain didn't have much time for religion. He

19

had an odd bundle of straw left over at the end of the winter, so he tossed it on the altar. "It should make a cheerful blaze, anyway", he said to himself. But Abel gave his sacrifice a lot of thought. In the end, he took his first and best lamb, and offered it to the Lord. The strange thing was, that while Abel's lamb cutlets burnt up completely, and smelt delicious, Cain's bundle of straw never caught light

20

at all. And that meant only one thing. God preferred Abel. Suddenly Cain flew into a rage. "Let's go for a little walk, shall we?" he said.

Once in the fields, Cain struck Abel to the ground and clubbed him to death with a heavy stone. Then he ran. When he paused for breath, he looked round cautiously. No one seemed to have noticed.

And then God spoke to him. "Hello, Cain. How's that brother of yours these days?" Cain shrugged. "How should I know? He's a big boy now. He can look after himself!"

And then the Lord said, "Cain, why did you do it? Don't you know that Abel's blood is shouting at Me, asking for revenge?"

Cain covered his face and fled. For the rest of his life he lived with the memory and guilt of what he had done. It was a fate worse than death.

Noah

The centuries rolled on. The number of people living on the earth steadily increased. Human nature being what it is, the world was far from being a happy place. Already people were quick to cheat. Already they were jealous of each other. Already the rich got richer at the poor man's expense. Sometimes God was sorry He had ever made Mankind.

But there was one person who always tried to do right. His name was Noah. He was a simple man who lived by farming. His hobby was carpentry, and he was fond of animals. Perhaps the most important thing about Noah was that he always took care to do things properly.

One day, God spoke to him. "Noah, I have decided to destroy mankind and start again. I'm tired of all the greed and violence. I can't bear to see it any longer."

Noah agreed. Things had got very bad. "How are you going to do it, Lord?" he said.

"I'm going to drown the world in a flood", said God. "Water will come in from the sea, and up from the wells, and down from the sky. No living creature will stand a chance."

"Will you destroy everything, Lord?" asked Noah. "Everything except you", said God.

In the months that followed, God taught Noah how to build a boat. It was called an Ark. It was 133 metres long, 22 metres wide, and 13 metres high. Noah's three sons helped him with the heavy work. They put in three decks and a door, and waterproofed it all with tar.

It really was a most ridiculous sight! A giant boat, standing hundreds of miles from the sea. People came from far and wide to look at it, and stood there laughing until the tears ran down their cheeks. But Noah wasn't to be put off. He had never seen rain, and he had never seen a flood, but he believed that such things were about to happen.

Then, one day, God told him to collect specimens of all living creatures. Any animals, reptiles, or birds he could find were to be brought into the safety of the Ark. "Now come aboard yourselves", said God. They did so. There were eight of them in all: Noah and his wife, and their three sons and their

23

wives. When they were all in, with the animals, and enough food to keep an army, they pulled the door shut. And then they waited for the rain.

"Any minute now", said Noah.

"You'd better believe it!" said his wife.

The Ark

It was a whole week before the rain began to fall. The rest of the family were all for admitting that they were wrong, and going back home. But Noah stood firm. "If God says there's going to be a Flood, there's going to be a Flood. So we're waiting in here if it takes a year!"

Meanwhile, the neighbours came to see how they were getting on. They knocked on the hull of the Ark. "Have you heard the long-range weather forecast?" they shouted. "Bright and sunny for the next six months!" They ran off, laughing as loudly as they could.

As it happened, they needed a week to get themselves organized. No one had any experience of running a small zoo, and there were quite a few problems to sort out. You could almost say they were teething troubles: like the lions showing their teeth at the cows, and the cats showing their teeth at

the mice! But somehow they managed to get all the enemies caged at opposite ends of the boat. After a while, Mrs Noah began to relax. She enjoyed the fresh milk from the goats, and the fresh eggs from the chickens. And she liked sitting down in the evening with her back against a donkey, and a lamb in her lap.

And then, one day, they heard an unfamiliar sound. Something soft was tapping on the roof. "That'll be the rain", said Noah, as though it happened every day. And it was. Soon it was falling quite fast. They looked out of the window at the puddles forming, and the people running for shelter. And then the lightning cracked and the thunder rolled and the storm began in earnest.

The amount of water was breath-taking. It

sheeted down as if barrels were being emptied from the sky. And it went on day after day after day. The neighbours who had come to laugh now hammered on the hull pleading to be let in. But it was too late. The mighty ship was already afloat.

For weeks the water grew deeper and deeper. Soon only the tops of the mountains were visible, crowded with people and animals. And then they too disappeared. The Ark was all alone, driven by the wind on the surface of the great Flood. Inside, Noah and his sons had their work cut out. No sooner had they got every animal fed, watered and cleaned out, than they had to start all over again. Only Mrs Noah had time to weep. She cried softly to herself when she thought of what had happened to the proud world outside, and all the people they had known.

About a month after their voyage had begun, the family were lingering over their evening meal. Suddenly, something seemed to be missing. Mrs Noah was the first to remark about it. "*Something* has stopped", she said. They looked at each other. Had a lion stopped snoring? Had a mouse stopped scratching? And then Noah realized what it was.

"It's the rain!", he cried. "Or rather, it's not the rain!" he added beaming all over his face.

The Rainbow

At first light, Noah lifted the hatch and looked out. In fact, the whole family wanted to peep – all at the same time. The fresh air was delicious! All around there was nothing but dark water and grey cloud. There was certainly no sign of land. Noah fetched a dove. He released it and watched it fly away. "That's one way of spying out the land", he said. "If the dove returns, we'll know there's not a dry spot anywhere yet." Sure enough, at nightfall the dove returned. She was nearly exhausted. She hadn't found a tree or rocky ledge in all her travels.

27

The entire world was still covered with water. Noah stretched out his hand, and brought the bird inside.

A week later, he released the dove again. They saw nothing of her all day. And then, in the evening, she came swooping down and alighted by the hatch. She had something in her beak. Noah looked more closely. The dove was carrying a fresh olive branch! It had found a tree-top, so the water must be going down. Everyone began to talk at once! Meanwhile, the dove sat looking puzzled. All she wanted to do was build a nest, but she couldn't do much with only one twig.

That night, the dove was guest of honour at dinner. The olive branch stood in a vase in the

middle of the table. Everyone thought it was more beautiful than any flower. It was the sign that God was making Peace. The sign that life would go on.

Noah waited another seven days. Once again he set the dove free and this time she did not return. Early next morning Noah slowly opened the hatch and stood with his wife. They blinked at the light of the rising sun. Soon they were joined by their family.

"Mud," said one of them, "nothing but mud."

"But it's land, and it's dry," said another, "and we're still alive!"

High overhead arched a beautiful rainbow. They looked at it in wonder. It was every colour under the sun, and perfectly formed. As they gazed, the Lord spoke:

"Noah, this bow is a sign.
I will never again destroy the earth.
As long as the world exists, there will be
   Summer and Winter,
   Seed-time and Harvest,
   Day and Night.
Whenever the sun shines through the rain
This bow will appear.
And I will remember My promise for ever."

The Tower

Once upon a time, everyone in the world spoke the same language. They used to live in tents, travelling from place to place, never really settling down. One day, some of them came to a great plain. It was wide and flat and fertile. "Let's stay here forever", said one of them. "Yes", said someone else. "Let's dig clay, bake bricks, and build lovely houses for ourselves. I'm tired of living in tents."

It seemed a good idea, and they all set to work. Other groups of shepherds joined them, until there was soon a bustling city. They called it Babylon. "This has really put us on the map", they said, patting each other on the back. "We've invented the very first city. We must be the centre of the world!" "Yes," they said, "the centre of the universe!" And they really began to believe it.

One day, the leaders held a meeting. A proud young man got up to speak. "My friends," he said, "we are the leaders of the world's first city. We are the greatest people that history has ever seen. I suggest we build a Tower as a memorial to ourselves. With our modern scientific knowledge, our perfect bricks, and our skilful engineering, we could build a Tower to reach the stars! The whole world will see our landmark."

An older man also rose to speak. "I don't know whether we shall reach the stars," he said, "but I like the idea, and I'll tell you why. When I was a little boy, my grandfather told me about a Flood. God was very angry with the peoples of the world, and sent a Flood to drown them. Only one family survived." He chuckled. "With this Tower, we'll

31

be safe if that should ever happen again. We'll be able to climb up into it, and stay there until the waters subside." He sat down to great applause.

And so the building began. The master builder drew a huge square on the ground, 100 metres by 100 metres. Bricks were made of clay, baked dry in the sun, and carried to the site in small carts pulled by donkeys. Then the bricks were hauled up the building in baskets. Tar was heated and poured between the bricks, to hold them together. When the walls of each storey were completed, the whole space was filled with earth, and stamped down ready for the next layer to be built. Higher and higher it rose. They invented ladders and scaffolding and hoists. And the work went even quicker.

It was a wonderful time. Everyone did their share. There were men for carting, men for hoisting, and men for laying bricks. As for the women, they busied themselves bringing fresh sandwiches and cool drinks to keep up the strength of the workers. They were all so full of themselves, and so certain of their success, that they made up a work song:

> "We are gods! We are gods!
> Look and be terrified
> We are gods!"

One day, God Himself came to look at the Tower. He was very impressed. Mankind must be learning very fast to be able to build to such a height without the whole thing collapsing. But then He heard the song! God was very angry. He didn't mind men growing in knowledge, but He hated their pride.

33

Even if they did reach the stars, at the end of the day they would still be sinful men. God said to Himself, "I must put a stop to all this, or there's no knowing where it will all lead."

At a stroke, He mixed up the language of all the people in Babylon. At first they looked helplessly from one to another. Then they began to quarrel. Fights began to break out . . . In the end, they gave up building the Tower, and many wandered away from the city to settle elsewhere.

And that was how God turned Babylon into Babble Town, and how the peoples of the world came to speak different languages.

Abraham Goes Berserk

It all started with the shop.

Abraham's father had a shop that sold gods. It was stacked from floor to ceiling with models and statuettes. There were gods of all shapes and sizes, and gods for every occasion. Big gods, little gods, fat gods, thin gods, gods to make your garden grow, gods to make your wife have babies, gods to stop burglars breaking into your house, gods to keep you safe on long journeys ... On one particular morning, Abraham was doing a roaring trade. And he hated every minute of it! He couldn't believe that these ugly lumps of wood had any power to help anyone. After all, they were only bits of carving knocked up by his father in the back yard ...

Finally, after the widow from down the road had spent her life's savings on a green monster with four arms, Abraham could stand it no longer. He ran along the shelves knocking all the idols to the floor, and then jumped on them. He felt a lot better straight away! He was still standing among the broken pieces, looking very pleased with himself, when his father walked in.

"Good heavens!" he said in astonishment. "Whatever's been going on here?"

"I'm afraid the gods went mad", said Abraham. "They were all so jealous when Widow Methuselah didn't choose one of them, that they turned on each other. Now they're all dead."

"You must be joking," said his father, "these idols can't do a thing. They're just bits and pieces I carve in the back yard."

"Exactly!" said Abraham in triumph. "You don't believe in them either. Well I'll tell you this, Dad, I'm not spending the rest of my life deceiving widows and taking their money. I believe in the Living God. He's not a god you can see, or turn into a doll. But He's real, and I'm going to spend the rest of my life in search of Him!"

*

"Just pack a few things", said Abraham to Sarah when he got home. "We're not staying here a day longer. I know we have a lovely house, and lots of friends, and we're near the shops. But the Living

God has told me to move. He's going to give us a new land somewhere. A land of our very own. And we're going to have children. Lots of children!"

Sarah was amazed. "I knew you were restless, Abraham, but I didn't realize it was as bad as that. It'll be exciting to see where God leads us, but you're wrong about the children. Anyway, let me help you pack."

At first light they were on their way. "No goodbyes", said Abraham. "If we start going round the neighbours it'll take all day, and they'll be so upset we'll change our minds and stay here after all."

"Where are you going, Uncle Abraham?" said a voice, as they tiptoed out of the gate. It was their nephew Lot. "Can I come too?"

"All right Lot. If you insist", said Abraham. "Let's go!"

Pharaoh's Little Mistake

They hadn't been gone long – only a few months. Abraham was having the time of his life. God showed them the lovely land of Canaan – well, it would be lovely when they'd dug some water wells and planted a few trees. They went from place to place, praying to the Living God.

But Sarah was far from pleased. "Promised Land?" she exploded at last. "It's a desert! Your Living God certainly likes a joke! Even the goats are getting skinny – and they can eat anything!"

Abraham had to admit that the new land was a big disappointment. There was very little grass for the animals, and he was feeling rather hungry himself.

"All right," he said, "I'll tell you what we'll do. We'll drop south to Egypt. There's always plenty of food there because they're right by the River Nile."

A few weeks later they arrived in Egypt. For

some reason the local boys kept turning round to look at them. "It must be because we're foreigners", thought Abraham, who had never been abroad before.

And then they started whistling!

"My goodness!" thought Abraham. "They're after my wife! She must be more beautiful than I thought."

He whispered to Sarah. "Look, darling, those whistles are for you. Take no notice. But if anyone asks you who you are, you'd better say you're my sister. I don't want to get killed for being your husband!"

"Thank you kindly, I'm sure" said Sarah.

★

The news of Sarah's beauty travelled like wild-fire. In no time at all (or so it seemed), an invitation came from His Serene Highness the Pharaoh. ("He's the local King", explained Abraham, as Sarah's general knowledge was very poor.)

39

"How wonderful!" said Sarah. "I'd love to meet the local King. You can come too, if you like", she added with a wink. "After all, you are my brother . . ."

*

They rode to the Palace in a state carriage, and arrived to find the banquet already spread. Sarah looked at the silver spoons and the golden goblets, and the roast lark's tongues, and the servants peeling grapes . . .

"Now this is what I call a Promised Land", she said to Abraham. "You can keep the desert."

Sarah was allowed to sit next to Pharaoh, and halfway through the meal (that is, after the fifth course) he gave her a priceless ring and kissed her hand. Sarah smiled at the Pharaoh. "It's so kind of you to welcome us like this, isn't it Abraham?"

Abraham swallowed some wine the wrong way, and his reply was lost in a fit of coughing.

Meanwhile, Lot was making the most of the chance to eat. "I say, these quails are very tasty, don't you think Uncle Abraham?" But Abraham's thoughts were elsewhere.

★

That night, in the royal guestrooms, the atmosphere was very awkward. Sarah broke the silence. "Darling, I think that nice King wants to marry me. Will you mind terribly if I accept?"

"Of course I'd mind!" said Abraham, thoroughly angry.

"Why can't I marry him?" said Sarah, sulkily.

"Because you're already married to me!" shouted Abraham at the top of his voice.

Well, of course, the chambermaid couldn't help but hear, especially as she was already listening behind the curtain. She told everyone in the

kitchens, and they told the waiters, and the waiters told . . . Well anyway, the news got back to Pharaoh, and he was very disappointed.

The following day, he summonded Abraham and Sarah to him. "My dear friend Abraham," he said, "I can't say how sorry I am. I really thought Sarah was your sister. Just think what your Living God would have done to me if I had stolen her."

Abraham was very confused. He didn't like admitting that it was his lie which had caused all the trouble. But Pharaoh went on, "Look, let me put things right. You want to start a new nation. So please accept a little gift of a few flocks and herds – and some servants to look after them. And then will you do me a favour? Get out of my sight as soon as possible!"

"I think we've upset him", said Abraham as they waved goodbye.

"But he's very polite, isn't he?" said Sarah.

Abraham looked behind him at the column of sheep and goats, cattle, donkeys, camels and slaves. He looked at his wife, riding beside him. He looked ahead at the desert road.

"The Living God has been very good, in spite of my mistake", he thought. "It makes me wish I'd trusted Him more!"

Lot's Choice

The years went by. Lot got married and had children. The servants got married and had children. The sheep and goats, cattle, donkeys and camels didn't bother to get married, but they certainly had children. To see Abraham and Lot going from place to place was like watching a small town on the move. Whenever they arrived at a well, there was a long queue for water, and a lot of jostling and bickering.

43

"Let me past, this is Abraham's bucket!"

"It wouldn't worry me if it belonged to the Man in the Moon! I was here first, and this is where I'm staying!"

One day Abraham took Lot to one side. "Look," he said, "we belong to the same family, so don't let's fight. I have an idea. You take one half of the Promised Land, and I'll take the other. Then we can each go our separate ways. Which half would you like?"

Lot looked east towards the sunrise. There was the most beautiful valley he had ever seen. The River Jordan ran clear and broad and sparkling through fertile meadows. He could see houses in the distance – white walls and shady gardens. He breathed a sigh.

"That's the place for me," he said, "I'm tired of this wandering life, living in tents and breathing in dust. I'll take the East Road".

So Abraham and Lot parted. Lot went to live near the cities of Sodom and Gomorrah. At first he only camped outside, but soon he bought himself a house and settled down with his family.

Abraham felt a tiny bit jealous that Lot had done so well out of the deal. But he knew it was right to give him first choice. And then the Living God spoke to him.

"Abraham, look around you. I'm going to give this land to you, as far as you can see in all directions! And don't worry about Lot having two daughters already. I'm going to give you so many grandchildren and great-grandchildren that people will lose count!"

"Thank you, Lord", said Abraham.

Hagar

Abraham and Sarah were getting old. Sarah's hair was going grey, and Abraham walked with a stick. One day they were sitting at the entrance of their tent, enjoying the cool of the evening. Abraham was very thoughtful.

"What's on your mind, darling?" asked Sarah.

"I was thinking about God," said Abraham, "and looking at the stars. You know, He once promised me I'd have so many children, that they'd be like sand on the sea shore and stars in the sky."

Sarah smiled, but sadly. "Sometimes I think you imagine these talks you have with God. We've lived and loved these many years, and you know we can't have children. I'm sorry. You're sorry. But there it is, and we must face facts."

They fell silent as their serving girl brought them drinks. Sarah looked at the girl. Her name was Hagar. She was young and strong, and quite good-looking.

45

When she had gone, Sarah said to Abraham, "Abraham, why don't you take another wife? Someone young and strong and quite good-looking. Then you can have children, and grandchildren, and great-grandchildren after all. I won't mind."

Abraham thought for a long time. Was this God's way? Some people *did* have more than one wife. Perhaps that serving girl – what was her name? Hagar. She was young and strong and quite good-looking – perhaps he could marry her. After all, she was already close to Sarah, and Sarah said she wouldn't mind . . .

So Abraham married Hagar, and in due course they had a son. They called him Ishmael, which means "God Hears". But no sooner did Hagar give Abraham a son than she became very proud. She looked down on Sarah, and Sarah was very upset. It's not much fun to be childless, especially when people think it's your fault.

Visitors

One baking-hot afternoon, when the glare of the sun and sand was almost unbearable, Abraham saw three figures coming towards him. He blinked and shielded his eyes. Yes, three strangers, moving in the heat of the day. Well, there was nothing for it, he'd have to get up and welcome them, perhaps invite them in for a meal. He ran to greet them, and bowed very low.

"Dear friends," he said, "this is warm weather for travellers. Please step inside my tent for a while. I'll bring water and food in no time, and then you can go on your way refreshed."

The strangers were delighted to accept. Soon they were sitting in the tent, eating and drinking, while Abraham waited on them. One of the men sat back with a sigh.

"Ah, that's better. Thank you, Abraham. By the way, do you have a wife?"

"Yes indeed," said Abraham, "her name is Sarah. I'm sorry to say we have no children."

"Well look here, Abraham", said the stranger. "You've been good to us. Let us do you some good in return. This time next year, your Sarah will give birth to a bouncing baby boy!"

Just then there was a muffled giggle from a dark corner of the tent. It was Sarah. She'd overheard the conversation, and it seemed too silly for words. It was very rude to laugh at strangers, so she immediately tried to turn it into a cough.

"What was that noise?" asked the stranger.

"That was Sarah", said Abraham. "I'm afraid she's so old now that the very idea of having children seems ridiculous. I must apologize."

"No, don't apologize", said the stranger. "It is the Living God who has promised you a son, and He will make sure it happens. Nothing is too hard for Him."

Just then, Sarah emerged. "I didn't laugh, you know," she said, "it was just a tickle in my throat."

"Oh you laughed all right", said the stranger. "But never mind. Carry on laughing. Laugh for joy that God is good to you! Mark my words, this time next year . . ."

Abraham decided to change the subject. "Where are you going?" he asked.

"We're on our way to Sodom", said the stranger. "We hear terrible things about what goes on there, and we're going to see if it's true."

Abraham shuddered. "It's true all right. I know because my nephew lives there. Do you have to go?"

The stranger looked at Abraham. "Abraham, I've decided to tell you something", he said. "We come from the Living God. He is angry with Sodom, and has decided to destroy the whole city. The people there are too evil to be allowed to live."

"But sir," said Abraham, thinking of Lot, "you might hurt innocent people. Not everyone's that bad. Supposing there are fifty good people in Sodom, would God spare the city?"

The stranger thought deeply. "Yes", he said. "The Living God would spare the city if there were fifty good men there."

But Abraham was still worried. For one thing, he wasn't at all sure that there *were* fifty good men in Sodom, not from what he'd heard. He plucked up courage and spoke again. He knew now that he was speaking to God. "My Lord, what if there are only forty-five good men? or only forty? or only – well, I'll be honest with you, Lord – supposing there are only ten good men in Sodom? Would you spare the city for the sake of those ten?"

This time the stranger didn't hesitate. "Abraham, you're daring to argue with God. I admire your boldness. If we find there are so many as ten good men in Sodom, we'll certainly spare the city for their sake."

And so the stranger left, with his two companions. "Ask for my nephew Lot!" Abraham called after them. "He's one good man for a start!"

Standing alone under the trees, with the evening drawing on, Abraham felt himself shaking all over. "There was something about those men", he said. "Something about them . . ."

50

Sodom

It was evening when the strangers arrived in Sodom. The air was very heavy. It was hard to move, hard to breathe.

Lot was sitting at the gate of the city. That was where the elders met to pass the time of day. Only Lot started up to meet the strangers.

"Forgive my friends", he said. "This is a rude and ruthless place. But my family still believe in making strangers welcome, so please stay the night at our house. We have food, water, and everything you need."

"Thank you", said the strangers. "We've already met your Uncle Abraham, and we know you are generous folk. But we've come to see what Sodom's *really* like, and that means we camp out in the square."

Lot was appalled. "Dear sirs, you've obviously no idea what goes on in this place. I can't begin to tell you how dangerous it is. Gangs roam the streets fighting each other and looking for trouble. Anyone by themselves is set upon and robbed. It doesn't matter whether you are man, woman or child, it's simply not safe to be out!"

In the end, the visitors gave in. They agreed to stay at Lot's house. They had a very good meal and were just getting ready for bed, when they heard shouting outside. Lot went deathly pale. "The gangs!" he whispered. He went to the window and peered through the curtains. The street was full of men brandishing torches.

"What do you want?" shouted Lot through the window.

"You know what we're after!" they yelled. "You've got some strangers in there, and we want them out here. We want to make them feel at home, don't we?" There was a great laugh from the mob. Lot took one more look at the leering faces, and drew the curtains tight shut.

"We've no time to lose", he said to the visitors. "Help me barricade the door!"

They placed all the furniture they could find against the door – tables, chairs, even a sideboard. Then Lot went upstairs to wake his wife and daughters.

"Quickly my dears, we're leaving just as we are. There's no time to pack. This way!"

As quietly as they could, they climbed out of a back window onto the flat roof. Then, under cover of darkness and the noise of the crowd, they slipped out of the city by a tiny side gate. Suddenly they noticed how hot it was.

"God is judging the city tonight!" said the strangers. "Run for your lives, and don't look back!"

With that, the ground leapt underneath their feet, and buildings began to sway. Trees were wrenched sideways, and left with their roots in the air.

"Don't just stand there – RUN!" So saying, the strangers turned back to the city to do their work.

Neither Lot nor his daughters could walk very far. They reached the little town of Zoar, and took cover. The sky over Sodom was full of fire and smoke. The whole valley was being filled with molten lava. Even from where they were, they could hear the screams of the dying.

And then they realized their own tragedy. Lot's wife had remembered something she'd left, and gone back for it. They never saw her again.

Ishmael

Abraham couldn't believe his ears. There was Sarah standing in front of him, beaming all over her face.

"Did you hear me, darling? I said I'm going to have a baby! You heard what the man said – this time next year!"

And so it was. Sarah gave birth to a baby boy, in spite of the fact that she was a very old woman. Their happiness was complete. She sat up in bed, with the child in her arms, and laughed for joy. The baby smiled too, though it may have been wind.

"Look at him, Abraham!" said Sarah. "Laughing all over his little face! We'll call him Isaac. That means 'Smiler'!"

But there was one person in camp who wasn't smiling, and that was Ishmael. He was jealous of baby Isaac, and started to give him sly pinches and kicks. One day Sarah saw what was going on, and had a word with Abraham.

"You know, Abraham, it's not going to work with two boys in the house. Ishmael may be the son of a slave, but he's your eldest. One day he's going to want a share of your money, and what happens to Isaac then?"

Abraham took the point. He was pacing up and down thinking about it, and wanting to do the right thing, when God spoke.

"Don't worry, Abraham", said God. "I have promised you grandchildren and great-grandchildren, and so you shall have. Isaac is the beginning of a whole nation. But Hagar and Ishmael must go away. I'll look after them. Ishmael is your son too, you know. I won't forget him."

★

Early next morning, Abraham gave Hagar some food and a bottle of water, and helped her strap Ishmael to her back. It hurt him more than he could say to send her off, but there are some times in life

55

when you can only do what God tells you to do.

After only a few days, the food and water ran out. Hagar lay Ishmael in the shade, and sat down some distance away.

"I can't bear to watch my child die", she said, burying her head in her hands, and bursting into tears. "So much for the God of Abraham!" she sobbed bitterly. "Telling my master to turn me out of house and home . . ."

And then she heard a voice, a voice which was very quiet, and very close.

"Don't worry, Hagar, I am with you. Pick up Ishmael and comfort him. I have plans for him too, you know!"

Slowly Hagar opened her eyes and looked up. Through her tears she saw a well nearby, and heard the laughter of women drawing water. She ran to fill her bottle, and took it to her little boy.

"Ishmael!" she whispered as she bathed his face and hands. "Ishmael, God loves us after all. We're going to live!"

Abraham's Greatest Test

The years rolled by. The seasons came and went.

Abraham's camp was now as big as a middle-sized town. Wherever he looked there were servants tending sheep, women cooking food, and children romping round the tents. And whenever he looked about, his gaze settled on Isaac. Isaac, his son. Isaac, the light of his life, the joy of his old age. Isaac, who would inherit all these servants and flocks when Abraham died.

One night God spoke. "Abraham!"

"Here I am, Lord", said Abraham, suddenly wide awake.

"Abraham, I want you to do something for me", said God.

"What is it, Lord?" asked Abraham.

And then God spoke. And as He spoke, Abraham was filled with dread.

"Abraham, I want you to prove your love for me by sacrificing Isaac. I want you to go three days' journey to Mount Moriah. I want you to build a fire on the flat rock there. I want you to lay Isaac on the fire on the rock, and kill him."

Abraham gave a deep groan and hid his face. To think that serving God should come to this!

"Lord, I am old and I've had a full life. Isaac is merely twelve, and has everything ahead of him. Please, take my life, and spare my son!"

But God said, "Abraham, if you love me, do it!"

The following day, the little party set out. They took two servants for protection, and a donkey to carry the firewood. Abraham carried an iron basket full of glowing charcoal, to light the fire when the time came.

Isaac leapt and danced ahead, delighted to be out with his Dad. Abraham followed slowly, deep in thought. Three days they travelled, stopping only to eat and sleep. And on the afternoon of the third day, they came to Mount Moriah. Abraham turned to the servants.

"You can wait here now", he said. "My son and I will go the rest of the way alone. He can carry the wood."

As they trudged towards the summit, Isaac broke the silence. "Excuse me Dad, but haven't you forgotten something?"

"What do you mean, my son?" said Abraham.

"Well, we're supposed to be offering a sacrifice to God. And we've got the knife, and we've got the fire, and we've got the wood . . . But where's the lamb?"

Abraham sighed and put his arm round Isaac's shoulders. "God knows about the lamb", he said.

They came to the flat stone. In the light of the setting sun, it was already blood-red. Abraham had been there many times over the years, to offer a bullock or a lamb in thanks to God. It had always been a solemn place, but never more solemn than it was today.

"Isaac," said Abraham, "I want you to do exactly as I say. Build the fire on the stone."

Isaac did so, slowly and carefully, feeling very honoured. He had never been present at a sacrifice before. But after all, he was twelve now. He was a man.

Abraham said, "Now Isaac, I'm going to bind your hands and feet and blindfold your eyes. Don't be afraid. You belong to the Living God. He gave you to me, and now He wants you back."

Tears were running down his cheeks. Gently, he lifted his son onto the pile of firewood, and reached for the knife to sharpen it. Isaac lay perfectly still.

Suddenly, Abraham took the knife in both hands, and lifted it high in the air. He paused. "Lord,

59

whether we live or die, we must do your will!"

And then God spoke. "Abraham! You can let Isaac go now. I know for sure that you love me more than your own life."

The summit was very quiet, just the song of a bird above, and the bleet of a ram nearby. The noise cut in on Abraham's thoughts. "A ram! What was a ram doing on Mount Moriah?"

Slowly he turned to look. Sure enough, there, caught by its horns in a thicket, was a solitary ram. With trembling fingers, Abraham put away his knife, untied Isaac and lifted him down. Together they caught the ram, bound it, killed it, and offered it to God.

As they re-traced their steps to find the servants, Isaac again broke the silence. "God knew about the sacrifice, didn't He Dad?"

"He did indeed, my son", said Abraham.

Lentil Soup

When Isaac was old enough, he married Rebecca. She was extremely beautiful, and he loved her very much. For many years they had no children at all. And then Rebecca gave birth to twins! The twins were born on the same day, but in every other respect they were completely different.

Esau (who was the elder by about a minute) had red hair and a ruddy skin. He grew up hairy and fierce, and loved the outdoor life. He was always in the hills or roaming the forest, and soon made his name as a hunter.

Jacob, on the other hand (he was the younger by that same fateful minute), was pale and weak. He liked nothing better than to stay at home with Mother and help her with the cooking. But he was very thoughtful. He thought about many things. And what he thought about most was that Esau was the elder, and that Esau would get God's blessing and the family fortune when their Father died.

One day, Jacob was quietly stirring some lentil soup when Esau rampaged in from one of his hunting trips. He tossed a dead hare in the corner, slapped Jacob on the back, and noisily sniffed the soup.

"My, that smells good!" he said, reaching for a spoon with his big hairy hand. "I do believe I'm about to die of starvation!"

Jacob thought quickly. "This is a little speciality of mine", he said. "It takes a long time to make, and is very expensive. I'll tell you what I'll do. I'll give you a bowl of my lentil soup, if you give me your title as the eldest son."

Esau threw back his head and laughed. Then he

gave Jacob a playful punch. Then he sat down with a thud.

"You mean I give you God's blessing and Dad's fortune, in exchange for a bowl of soup?" he said, unable to believe Jacob was really serious.

"That's right", said Jacob, smiling sweetly.'

Suddenly Esau's face cleared, and he laughed again. "Done! so far as I am concerned, you're welcome to God's blessing *and* the family fortune. I'd rather have lentil soup any day!" And with that, he took a hunk of bread in one hand and a ladle in the other, and enjoyed a hearty meal.

"It may never happen anyway," he said with his mouth full, passing his plate for more.

The Lie

Isaac was very old. His sight was fading. When he was indoors, he could hardly see at all. One day he called Esau to see him.

"Esau," he said, "I'm an old man and I haven't long to live. The time has come for me to pass on God's blessing to you. It's a very special blessing, and I can only give it once."

"Thank you, Father", said Esau.

Isaac went on. "Listen, Esau. Before I give you the blessing, take your bow and arrows, and kill me a buck. We'll celebrate today with a nice dish of venison – you know, the way I like it!"

Esau's eyes lit up. "It'll be a pleasure, Father", he said. And off he went.

*

No sooner had Esau disappeared, than Rebecca slipped out to find Jacob. She'd been listening from behind a curtain, and knew exactly what she'd do.

"Jacob," she said, "today's the day your Father will give his final blessing. It's a very special blessing, and it can only be given once. Now listen! We'll dress you up as Esau, cook a tasty dish of lamb – it'll be so spicy he'll never know it's not venison – and by the time Esau's back, the blessing will be yours!"

"But Mother," said Jacob, "Esau's a big strong hairy chap. His voice is deep, and he smells of the open air. Father will know I'm not Esau!"

"No he won't," said Rebecca, "I'll see to that."

And so she did. She stuck goatskin on Jacob's

arms, lent him some of Esau's sweaty clothes to put on, and ruffled his hair. Then she gave him a bowl of spiced lamb, together with some fresh bread.

"Now get in there", she said. "And don't come out until you've got the blessing!"

★

"Is that you, Esau?" said Isaac, when he heard Jacob come in.

"Yes, Father", said Jacob in a gruff voice, which didn't sound a bit like Esau, but it was the best he could do.

"Are you back already?" asked Isaac. "You haven't been gone five minutes."

"This is a special day, Father," said Jacob, "God gave me a kill straight away."

"He seems to have given you a sore throat too", said Isaac. "You sound more like Jacob to me. Anyway, come here where I can touch you."

Jacob went over and sat down beside his Father. Isaac reached out and felt his tousled hair.

"Well, I don't know," he said, "you sound like Jacob and you smell like Esau. Let me see your arms." Isaac ran his fingers over the goatskin on

66

Jacob's arms. "Yes, there's no doubt about your arms anyway," he said, "those are Esau's arms all right – hairy as an old goat!" And he laughed. "But tell me, on your honour," he said, "are you really Esau?"

"Yes, I am", said Jacob.

"All right then," said Isaac, "give me that tasty meal, and when I've finished, I'll give you my blessing."

So Isaac ate the tasty meal. And after he had eaten, he laid his hands on Jacob's head, and said these solemn words.

"The God of Abraham and Isaac bless you!
May He send dew on your fields and make your land rich.
May He give you plenty of corn and wine!
May all go well for you,
and for those you love, both now and for ever more."

"Amen", said Jacob, but his voice still didn't sound right, so he pretended he was just clearing his throat.

"Well, that's that", said Isaac. "You now have God's special blessing. It's yours to pass on to your children for ever."

★

Some time later, Esau came in to see Isaac, and brought with him a steaming plate of venison. Isaac had been nodding off. He was annoyed at being woken up. "Take that stuff away!" he said. "I've eaten very well already, thank you."

"But Father, it's me! Esau! I've brought you the venison – you know, cooked the way you like it . . ?"

67

His voice trailed off as he realized something was terribly wrong. Isaac's jaw dropped, as the truth dawned on him, too.

"Esau," he said, his words a mere whisper, "I'm afraid to say that Jacob has stolen your blessing." He was trembling. "It's a very special blessing, and I can only give it once . . ."

Esau dropped the plate of venison and ran to his Father. "But Father! That's not possible! Tell me it's not true . . ." Esau was a brave man, but now he began to cry.

"All right, my son," said Isaac, "here is a blessing for you." He laid his hands on Esau's head, and said these solemn words.

> "My son, you will find life hard.
> The dew won't fall on your fields.
> Your land may not be rich.
> You will live by the sword,
> And become your brother's slave.
> But in the end,
> Yes, in the end, you will be free!"

As Esau got up and left his Father's tent, there was only one thought in his mind – revenge!

Jacob's Ladder

Jacob had been on the run for several days. He headed north through the hills of Palestine, with Esau's threats still ringing in his ears. Cold, lonely, and far from home, he stopped for the night. He had never been away before. He missed the sounds of the camp site, the smell of cooking, and the glow of the night fires. He shivered and drew his cloak about him. He chose a large stone for a pillow, lay down, and went to sleep.

As he slept, he dreamed. He dreamed that the rocky land around him became a giant stairway, a stairway which rose from earth to heaven. And on that stairway were God's messengers, going to and fro on God's business.

Suddenly God seemed very close. Jacob had never thought much about God before. He knew that God meant a lot to some people, but somehow God had never meant much to him. And then Jacob heard someone speaking to him.

"Jacob, I am the Lord. I was with your grandfather Abraham, and your father Isaac, and now I want to be with you. I will keep you safe on your journey, and one day I will give you this very ground on which you are lying. In fact it will all be yours, as far as you can see. That's a promise!"

★

When Jacob woke up the following morning, the dream was still very vivid. He shook his head and rubbed his eyes, but the voice wouldn't go away. So there and then, Jacob took the stone he had used as a pillow, and turned it into an altar. And he prayed to the Living God.

"Lord God, if you are really here, then help me to make a new start in life. I'm a young man, alone in the world, and without a home or a job. If you will help me now, then I shall certainly worship you."

With that, he went on his way. He crossed the river Jabbok, and turned east towards the rising sun. He was looking for a place called Haran, the home of his Mother's brother – known to the family as Uncle Laban.

70

Rachel

It was several days later when Jacob came in sight of a well. Three flocks of sheep were already there to be watered, but the shepherds were obviously waiting for others to arrive.

"Good day", said Jacob. "Could you tell me the name of this place?"

"This is Haran", said the shepherds.

"That's marvellous!" said Jacob. "Do you know a man called Laban? He's my uncle."

"We know Laban all right", said the shepherds. But before Jacob could ask anything further, one of them said, "Look out, here's his daughter!"

And that was how Jacob met Rachel. She arrived with her flock of sheep, and looked helplessly at the boulder which covered the well. None of the shepherds made a move.

"Here, let me shift that stone for you", said Jacob. It was quite a job for someone who never did any work, but his journey had toughened him up a bit. At last the stone rolled back, and he gallantly bucketed out some water for the sheep.

Rachel seemed impressed. She smiled at him shyly. Jacob looked at her. She had very beautiful eyes. While they were watering the animals, Jacob introduced himself.

"My name is Jacob," he said, "I've come all the way from Beersheba to find your Father. You see, I'm your cousin."

Well of course Rachel was delighted, and Jacob took the opportunity of kissing her. Then she ran all the way home.

When Laban heard that a nephew had arrived, he came hurrying out to meet him. He was a little man, with crafty eyes – in fact he looked like nobody more than Jacob! Anyway, Jacob was given the warmest of welcomes, and invited to stay for as long as he liked.

Leah

There followed the happiest month of Jacob's life. He worked harder than all the other shepherds put together (which wasn't saying very much). But more than that, he was free of his mother's apron-strings, and he was safe from his brother's revenge. And even more than that, he could see Rachel every day.

But Rachel wasn't Laban's only daughter. There was her elder sister, Leah, as well. She had very beautiful eyes, but the rest of her was rather angular and awkward. Jacob definitely preferred Rachel.

One day, Laban and Jacob had a heart-to-heart talk. Laban didn't want to lose Jacob, because he was such a good worker. Jacob didn't want to leave Laban, because he loved being near Rachel. So they agreed that Jacob should sign on as apprentice for seven years, and at the end of that time he could have Rachel for his wife. Jacob was overjoyed.

The seven long years simply flew by, so happy was he in his work and in his love. At last the great day arrived, and Uncle Laban provided a surprisingly generous feast. When everyone was getting merry, and the lights were low, the bride arrived. She was stunningly beautiful. At least, her clothes were stunningly beautiful. It was rather hard to see the bride herself, because of the large number of veils, shawls and scarves that she was wearing.

Well, of course, the bride wasn't Rachel at all. But it wasn't until the following morning that Jacob discovered the trick. Jacob leapt from his bed in a towering rage, and went in search of Laban.

"You twister!" he yelled. "You deceived me! Seven long years I've worked for you, and you play a trick like this!"

"Now calm down, old chap", said Laban. "It's not as bad as all that. I can't have you carrying off my prettiest daughter, leaving me with an elderly spinster to support. So I've given you Leah first." He patted Jacob on the arm. "I'll tell you what I'll do. If you work for me another seven years, I'll give you Rachel as well. What do you say?"

Free at Last

Things were never the same again between Jacob and Laban. They couldn't trust each other, because they were two of a kind!

One day Jacob said to his uncle, "I've worked fourteen years for you. I came with nothing. Now I have two wives, eleven sons, and a daughter. And you haven't done so badly out of the deal. Your flocks have become the largest in the area since I took over. But now you must let me go."

But Laban couldn't afford to lose Jacob. "What can I do to persuade you to stay?" he said.

"Well," said Jacob, "if you're really making me an offer, give me all the goats with spots or stripes, and all the black sheep. You can keep the pure white animals for yourself."

Laban agreed. Of course, being unable to keep any sort of bargain, he immediately sent his sons off with all the spotted and striped goats and all the black sheep! But Jacob had expected as much . . .

Nevertheless, over the next few years, with very careful breeding, Jacob built up a fine herd of his own. True, they weren't very good-looking. But their fleece was good, and their milk was good, and they were very hardy.

Jacob decided the time had come to leave. And they must leave in a hurry – no more bargains, no more tricks. So it was that, early one morning, Jacob, Rachel and Leah, with their children, slaves,

flocks, camels, and donkeys, left Haran without
bothering to say goodbye. It was ten days later
when Laban caught up with them. By that time they
were in the hills of Gilead.

"Why did you walk out, just like that?" asked Laban, still breathless from the chase, "I only wanted to kiss everyone goodbye." He looked shrewdly at Jacob. "No doubt you've stolen something", he said. "Let me search your baggage!"

He turned all their bundles and baskets inside out, and Jacob was furious. Actually, they had stolen some of Laban's idols and magic charms, but he didn't find them because Rachel was sitting on them! Finally Laban gave in.

"All right," he said, "you can go. I've given you twenty years of my life, and you've taken my daughters, my grandchildren, and the bulk of my flocks." He shrugged. "But I can see you don't love me any more, and you want to go back home, so God be with you."

Maybe he expected them to change their minds. But they didn't. When Jacob had gone, Laban turned for home by himself. The old cheat had finally met his match.

Wrestling with God

The time was drawing near when Jacob would have to meet Esau. The very prospect made him shudder! He prayed as he had never prayed before.

"God of Abraham and Isaac! You promised me safety, and a land of my own. When I came this way before, I had nothing but a walking stick. Now I have this huge family. But Esau is heading this way with his army. Lord, save us!"

He thought hard. He decided to break his party into small groups, and send them on ahead. If Esau met them, they were to say that they were a present from Jacob. If one of the groups was attacked, at least some others might escape.

78

Jacob was pacing up and down, deep in thought, when he felt a hand on his shoulder. He swung round, but the stranger held on. Jacob ducked quickly, trying to throw the stranger over his head. They both fell to the ground, fighting.

They wrestled throughout the night. The stranger was strong, but Jacob was determined. As dawn began to break, the stranger struck Jacob's hip, sending a shooting pain down his leg. But Jacob refused to be beaten. In fact, he fought harder, despite the pain.

In the end, the stranger cried, "It's getting light! Let me go!"

Jacob hung on. "I will not let you go! Not unless you bless me . . ."

"What is your name?" asked the stranger.

"Jacob", he replied.

"Well, Jacob," said the stranger, "I'll give you a new name. From now on you shall be called 'Israel'. It means 'He who struggles'! You're a fighter, Israel. You fight with men, and you fight with God!" And so saying, the stranger left him.

As the sun came up, Jacob limped away from Peniel. He crossed the River Jabbok, and went to face Esau.

"After all," he said to himself, "I've just seen God, and I'm alive to tell the tale. What more can Esau do to me?"

But lo and behold, when Jacob and Esau did meet, they fell into each other's arms!

Joseph

Esau and Jacob got on quite well after that. They were both older and wiser, and knew that fighting makes life a misery. Esau had four wives and six sons, and moved away to live in the hills.

Meanwhile Jacob had two wives, two mistresses, and eleven sons! Although he never wanted to marry Leah, she was in fact the mother of six strapping lads – half the children of Israel! As for Rachel, she had no children at all for many years, and then gave birth to Joseph.

81

Joseph was just like his dad – spoilt. Maybe Jacob was getting old. Maybe he was going soft. But he made far too much fuss of his youngest son. The others hated it. Matters got worse when Jacob presented Joseph with a most beautiful coat. It was all the colours of the rainbow, and it had fine, billowing sleeves. It was the sort of coat you'd give to a prince. At the age of seventeen, Joseph looked far too smart to be living in a shepherds' camp.

Not surprisingly, he began to dream. He began to get ideas. And, rather unwisely, he told his brothers all about them! "I had a wonderful dream last night", he would say, as he strolled in late for breakfast. "We were all tying bundles of corn, when suddenly my bundle stood up straight, and all your bundles gathered round and bowed to it! What do you think of that?" Well, in those days, people attached a lot of importance to dreams. And Joseph's brothers didn't think too much of it at all!

Another morning he didn't arrive for breakfast until they were all clearing away. "Sorry I'm late," he said casually, "I've been having one of my dreams again."

"What were you this time?" sneered Judah, "the sun, moon and stars?"

"That's quite a good guess", said Joseph, with a superior smile. "Actually, Father was the sun, Mother was the moon, and you were the stars."

"And where were you?" asked Simeon.

"I was myself, and you were all bowing down to me again", said Joseph.

"I could ring his silly neck!" muttered Levi to Reuben.

Joseph is Sold

One day, when the ten brothers had gone far from camp to find pasture for the flocks, Jacob called Joseph to him.

"My son," said the old man, "I'm worried about those boys. Could you go in search of them, see how they are, and come back and tell me?"

"All right", said Joseph. He put on his fine coat, and set out.

The brothers saw him coming a mile off. There was no one else in the Middle East who went out walking in a coat like that. The sun caught the colours and the wind caught the sleeves. Here was the chance they'd been waiting for.

"This is it, lads", said Judah. "Gather round!"

They strolled towards Joseph, smiling grimly. "Welcome, Prince Joseph!" said Simeon, with a flourish. "How are Your Majesty's feet after Your

Majesty's walk?'' said Levi, bowing low, and spitting. ''Had any good dreams lately?''

By this time they were crowding Joseph, bumping and jostling him. They had his fancy coat in no time, and ripped off the sleeves. Then Levi produced a knife. ''All right, let's settle him once and for all!''

But Reuben stepped between them. "No! We'll not kill him. I'm the eldest, and Father would never forgive me. We'll throw him into this dry pit, and leave him to learn some manners." And so they did.

While they were eating the food Joseph had brought, and laughing at his cries from the well, a caravan of merchants drew up. The brothers smiled as they watched them go to the well and find, not water, but one very hot and bothered young man! While Reuben was away checking the herd, the rest of the brothers went over to the traders. They took a rope with them and hauled Joseph out of the pit.

"You can have him for twenty-five," said Judah to the Arabs.

"Twenty!" said the Arabs, who weren't traders for nothing. "Done!" said Judah. "Now take him quickly before Big Brother comes back!"

They handed Joseph to the merchants and watched as he was roped to a camel. "Good luck in Egypt", said Simeon. "Good luck, and sweet dreams!"

When Reuben returned and found Joseph gone, he tore his clothes in dismay. He rounded on the others. "And what am I supposed to tell Father?"

"No need to tell him anything," said Levi, who had it all worked out. He had killed a goat, and was busily daubing Joseph's coat in blood. "Just tell Dad we found this on the road."

And that is what they did. When Jacob saw it, he wept for many days. "There's no doubt about it, the coat is Joseph's!" He held the tattered garment to him, and cried aloud, "My son! My son! If only I could have died instead!"

At Potiphar's House

Once in Egypt, Joseph was sold to Captain Potiphar, who was on the Palace Staff. Potiphar soon realized he had a bargain. Joseph could read and write, and was an excellent organizer. Soon he was running the household, and Potiphar was content to leave everything to him.

And then there was Mrs Potiphar. She had been good-looking in her time, though now she was past her best. What's more, she was lonely, with the Captain out all the time. Lonely – and bored. The only interest in her life was Joseph. She enjoyed having him around the house. One evening, she called him to her room.

"Joseph, you look tired. Why not sit down for a minute and have a quiet drink?"

"Thank you very much, Madam," said Joseph, "but I have a lot to do."

Mrs Potiphar pretended to be stern. "Now listen, young man. I give the orders in this house, and I'm telling you to look after me this minute!" She put her arms round Joseph's neck, and lifted her face to be kissed.

Joseph blushed. "But Madam! You're married to my Master – you shouldn't be doing this!" He tried to get away. She clung to him so tightly, that in the end he had to leave his jacket in her hands. He fled from the room.

Well, when the Captain came home, there was his wife, and there was the drink, and there was Joseph's coat!

"What on earth's been going on?" he said, rushing to her side.

"Oh darling," she said, "something terrible has happened. That fine Joseph you think so much of – he came in here as soon as you'd gone out, and forced himself on me. I resisted him, and in the end he ran away, leaving his coat. But he'll have to go!"

And the Captain believed her. Not only was he very upset at what had happened, he was also angry with himself for having trusted a foreigner in the first place. Without more ado, he had Joseph thrown into prison.

Pharaoh's Dream

Meet Pharaoh Rameses. That's him with the beard.
That's his wife with the curlers. They are asleep. At
least, they are trying to sleep. But Pharaoh keeps
having nightmares. He mutters and moans, and
even cries out.

"What's the matter?" asks his wife anxiously.

"I keep dreaming of cows. Fat cows and skinny
cows. I know it sounds silly, but there's something
frightening about them." He sits up and pulls the
bell rope.

At once, all his wise men and advisers come
stumbling in, rubbing their eyes. They are always
on call. They gather at the foot of the bed.

"What do you make of this one?" says Rameses.

"There are seven cows, sleek and fat, grazing on the banks of the river. Then along come seven mangy cows, with ribs poking through their hides. And they gobble up the fat ones! I tell you, it's really scary!"

Well, the wise men and advisers scratch their heads and stroke their beards, but they can't make any sense of the dream at all. The butler comes in with a cup of warm milk for Pharaoh. In passing, he says, "Your Excellency, there's a man called Joseph in prison here. He's very good at explaining dreams. He did mine for me, and it all came true!"

"Bring him here!" says Pharaoh.

So Joseph is brought from prison in the early hours of the morning, and Pharaoh tells him all about the dream. The Living God tells Joseph what it means, and Joseph tells Pharaoh.

"Your Excellency," he says, "the land of Egypt will enjoy seven years of good weather and fine harvests. These are the seven fat cows. But then will come seven years of drought, crop failure and hunger. These are the seven thin cows."

"Of course!" says Pharaoh. "Of course! It stands out a mile now you tell me!" And then his face falls. "But what are we going to do?"

"If I may be so bold," says Joseph, "I would suggest that Your Excellency puts the situation in the hands of someone he can trust. Someone who will organize storage depots during the good years, and manage the rationing during the famine."

"Brilliant!" says Pharaoh, brightening straight away. "Joseph, you have just talked yourself into a job!"

Prime Minister

So it was that, at the age of thirty, Joseph became Prime Minister. Pharaoh had him fitted out with a fine linen robe, and put a ring on his finger and a gold chain round his neck. He also presented him with a royal chariot, which was only one size smaller

than his own. Wherever he went, Joseph was preceded by a Guard of Honour, shouting, "Make way! Make way!" This appealed to Joseph who, you will remember, had always had big ideas.

The years of plenty came and went. Joseph built special barns in all the cities, and carefully stored the surplus grain. And then came the famine. The rivers dried up, and the sun beat down for seven parched years.

It wasn't only Egypt that suffered. People came from all over the world to buy grain, when they heard of Joseph's barns. And among the groups thronging into Egypt was (you guessed?) a travel-stained band called the Sons of Jacob! Mind you, not all of them were there. Rachel had had a second son, Benjamin, before she died. Jacob wouldn't let him out of his sight, in case he lost him.

One day, Joseph was supervising the sale of corn, when he saw his brothers in the queue. He was deeply moved to see them, but they didn't recognize him. He decided to be business-like. "Name?"

"We are the Sons of Jacob from Canaan, Your Highness", they said, squirming and crawling.

"I think you're a bunch of thieves!" said Joseph sharply. "Are you all here?"

"All except one, Your Highness", said Reuben. "We have a little brother, Benjamin, but our Father has kept him at home."

"I don't believe that, for a start", said Joseph.

"Well, we did have another brother once. Joseph. But he disappeared. We lost him."

"Just like that?" said Joseph. The brothers shifted uneasily. Joseph went on. "It's my opinion that you're spies. I'm going to hold you in prison for three days. Then I want you to prove your story by going and bringing back Benjamin. Meanwhile, I'll keep one of you here as hostage. I'm not stupid, you know!" With that, Joseph left the room, and laughed until he cried.

Meanwhile the brothers were muttering to each other. "This is a judgement on us," said Reuben, "a punishment for what we did to Joseph. I knew God wouldn't let it pass."

96

Happy Ending

Jacob listened to the story his sons had to tell. He looked very old, very tired.

"You mean the Prime Minister of Egypt wants to see Benjamin?" he said for the tenth time. "Why on earth did you even mention that you had another brother?" he wailed. "This will be the death of me . . ."

In the end hunger got the better of them. Jacob had to agree that Benjamin should go with them to Egypt, to get more food. When they arrived, they were sent straight to the Prime Minister's house. "He's expecting you for supper", said a servant. And sure enough, when they arrived at the Prime Minister's house, there was Joseph with a feast all prepared. The brothers could hardly believe their eyes.

"So," said the Prime Minister, "you've come back after all. And this must be young Benjamin. How's your old father, Benjamin? Still alive?" The brothers looked at each other in amazement. This Prime Minister had a wonderful memory for names!

They ate and drank, and went to bed very late. In the morning they woke to find a sackful of grain for each of them, and the donkeys loaded ready for the journey. "Goodbye!" said Joseph, trying not to laugh. He managed to keep a straight face until they had disappeared round the corner. Then he turned to his Head Servant.

"Quick! Get after them. Search their sacks. You'll find my silver cup hidden in Benjamin's grain. Charge them with theft, and bring them back here!"

Sure enough, right at the bottom of Benjamin's sack, was Joseph's favourite goblet. "I must ask you to come with me!" said the Head Servant, in his best policeman's voice.

Back at the Palace, Joseph could keep the secret no longer. He took one look at his brothers grovelling and apologizing, and promising never to do it again. Then he sent the servants from the room.

"Listen," he said, "I am Joseph – the brother you thought was dead!" Nobody moved. Joseph held out his hands to them. "It's true! You sold me as a slave, but only because God let you. It was God's way of getting us to Egypt, so that we'd all survive the famine!" And then, with the tears rolling down their cheeks, they shook hands and embraced each other.

The Hebrews

It took some months to get the good news back to Jacob, and bring all their families in wagons down into Egypt. The Pharaoh gave them a warm welcome, and said they could look after their herds in Goshen.

Years passed by. Jacob, Joseph, and all the brothers died. Pharaohs came and went. And all the time the families lived in Goshen. And all the time there were more of them! They became known as "The Hebrews".

One day, the newest Pharaoh made a big speech. "My dear people," he said (which was always a sign that he was about to say something nasty), "my dear people, I'm worried that we have so many Hebrews living in our land. They're not true Egyptians, and they might some day turn against us. So from now on, I declare that they shall be slaves. They must be made to build pyramids and treasure cities. And if they refuse to work, whip them hard!"

So the Hebrews fell into slavery. Their lives were a misery from dawn to dusk. Goshen became a shanty town where they ate dry bread and snatched a little sleep. And yet their numbers continued to grow! The Pharaoh tried again.

"My dear people," he said ("Wait for it," thought everyone, "here it comes!"), "my dear people, I don't like the way the Hebrews are growing in number. So, to put an end to the problem, I declare that all baby boys must be thrown in the river!"

Well, there was one Hebrew mother who was more than a match for Pharaoh. She had a baby boy who was three months old. "If my baby has to go in the river, so be it," she said to herself, "but I'm going to make him a boat first!"

Carefully she wove a basket of reeds, coated it with tar to make it watertight, and laid her baby safely inside. Then she placed the basket gently in the rushes by the side of the river, and left her daughter Miriam to keep watch. They had no doubt that God would do something. But what?

Water Baby

After a while, Miriam heard someone approaching. It was a group of girls. One of the girls was none other than Pharaoh's daughter!

As it turned out, only the Princess went for a swim that day. "Hey!" she called to her friends, "There's a little basket bobbing in the rushes. Try to get it for me!"

They waded in and picked up the basket. With great excitement, they clustered round. And there, blinking in the daylight, was a baby Hebrew.

Just then Miriam strolled out of the undergrowth. She was whistling to herself, and seemed startled when she saw the Princess. "Oh, is that a baby?" she said, running up to take a look. "Are you going to keep him? Do you want a nurse?"

The Princess smiled. She rather liked the Hebrews. "Yes, little girl. I'm going to look after this baby, and I would be most grateful if you could find him a nurse. Bring her to the Palace, and say I asked you to come."

So . . . you guessed? Miriam went and brought her mother to the Palace, and she looked after her own baby! The Princess adopted the boy, and called him "Moses". He was soon learning to read and write, and the Princess taught him the best Egyptian manners. At the same time, his real mother made sure he knew all about the Hebrews. She never let him forget that his people were slaves.

Murder!

Moses grew tall and strong. He was a Prince among Egyptians. He studied in the royal libraries, and feasted at the Pharaoh's table. But somehow he never felt really at home in the Palace. He didn't know why.

One day he thought he would take a look at the Hebrews. He had heard that they were a noble people. He knew that they worshipped the Living God. And, after all, he was a Hebrew himself by birth. That was what his nurse had told him. Moses wandered down towards Goshen, the excitement mounting within him. And then he saw them.

Hundreds and hundreds of naked slaves, trying to make bricks out of clay and straw. Even from where he was, he could hear the brutal shouts of the Egyptian taskmasters, and the cracking of the whips. Moses was dumbfounded. The Hebrews were a noble people. They served the Living God. How had they ever become slaves?

Then, before his very eyes, Moses saw one of the Egyptian taskmasters take a Hebrew by the throat. He threw the slave to the ground and repeatedly kicked him and lashed him with a whip. Without thinking, Moses ran over and felled the Egyptian with a single blow. He was so angry that he didn't know what he was doing. He seized the whip and

started to beat the Egyptian. "I'll teach you to respect the Hebrews!" he shouted. The man was on the ground, but Moses didn't stop. He went on hitting the Egyptian and screaming at the top of his voice, until there was a silence. Then the red fog of his anger began to melt away. He looked down at the Egyptian. He was dead. Stone dead. Hurriedly, Moses buried the man in the sand. He looked round to see if anyone was watching. Then he ran for his life.

In no time the news was everywhere. Prince Moses is a Hebrew! He has murdered an Egyptian! The Pharaoh put out a warrant for his arrest. But it was too late. Moses had gone.

On the Run

At first Moses fled to Goshen. He wanted to hide with the Hebrews, share their life, and learn their ways, but they didn't trust him. They were suspicious of his Egyptian clothes. And they knew about the murder . . . When a quarrel broke out between two Hebrews, and they drew knives, Moses tried to stop them. They turned on him. "Who do you think you are, Pharaoh's pet! Go back to your basket in the Palace! Or would you like to kill us too?"

Moses looked at them in horror. He wasn't at home in the Palace, but he wasn't welcome here either. He turned and fled again.

That night he travelled east, using dangerous roads, flooded at high water. Then for many days he wandered in the desert without food. The jackals lurked nearby, and the vultures hung overhead ... waiting for him to die. But Moses didn't die. Instead, he found a well. And near the well were a number of girls, getting water for their animals. Moses started to help them.

It turned out that they were the seven daughters of Jethro, who was the local priest. They came to draw water every day, but had never had help from anyone before. Their father was amazed when they arrived home early. "A man called Moses helped us, Father," said Zipporah, "he's a stranger in these parts." "Then bring him here", said Jethro. "He shall stay with us for as long as he likes."

The Bush

Moses lived in Midian for forty years. He learned how to tend sheep, find water, fight wild animals, and steer by the stars. He was a shy man, but he managed to pluck up courage to propose to Zipporah, and together they had a son. They called him "Foreigner", because Moses still didn't feel at home.

He loved to talk to his father-in-law. Jethro told him more about the Living God, and told him the old tales of Abraham, Isaac and Jacob.

One day, Moses was feeding his sheep on the slopes of Mount Horeb, when he saw a remarkable sight. Nearby, a bush had burst into flame. Well, there was nothing unusual in that, because the sun was very fierce. The astonishing thing was that the bush wasn't in fact burning! It was standing, unharmed, in the midst of the blaze. And then Moses heard the Voice. And that was when he began to get really worried.

"Take off your sandals, Moses. You are standing in the presence of God!"

Moses hurriedly kicked off his shoes, and fell to the ground. He had heard a lot about the Living God, but to meet Him face to face was quite another matter.

"Moses," said God, "the time has come to rescue

the Hebrews from Egypt. They've been slaves there
long enough."

"But how are you going to rescue them, Lord?"

110

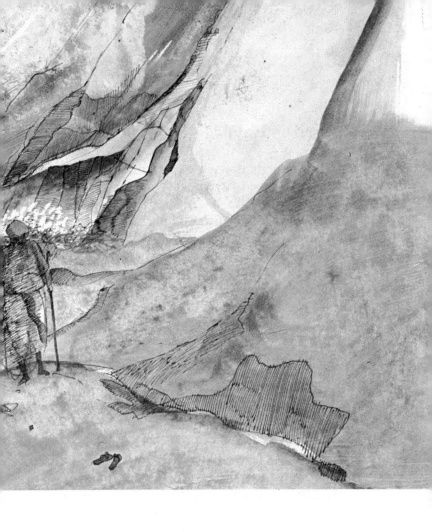

said Moses. "They'll need a leader to persuade them, and they'll need signs to convince them."

"That's where you and I come in", said God.

Return to Egypt

On the long road back to Egypt, Moses and his family happened to meet Aaron. Aaron – his brother, whom he hadn't seen for years. They greeted each other with open arms.

"What brings you this way?" asked Aaron, "I was just on my way to see you!"

"The Living God is sending me back to Egypt", said Moses. "I must tell Pharaoh to set the Hebrews free!" Aaron was most impressed. "But you must come and do the talking. I'm so shy, and I have such a stutter, that I'll never persuade Pharaoh. But you're a great speaker. God will tell me what to say, and I'll tell you!"

It sounded a funny arrangement, but Aaron agreed.

*

Once they were back in Egypt, they went to call on Pharaoh. The Hebrews were being as badly treated as ever, and their future looked very black.

At last a servant appeared. They were shown into the throne room. It was pleasant enough, with a window overlooking the building works. Pharaoh looked very daunting, wearing all his finery and sitting on a high chair at the top of a flight of steps.

Aaron didn't wait. He blurted out the speech as soon as he got into the room. It tumbled out higgledy-piggledy, and Moses wished he'd done the job himself – which is what God had wanted in the first place.

"Our God is the God of the Hebrews. To honour the God of our forefathers, there is always a three-day feast in the desert. We therefore beg you, great Pharaoh, to let our people go, so that they may attend this feast."

The Pharaoh remained silent for quite a while. In fact they wondered if he'd heard them. And then he said, "It always interests us to hear of a new god. We like to write them down in a book. Now let me see," he said, "how do you spell this one's name?"

Aaron drew breath to reply, but Moses interrupted. "Great King, our God has no name. He is who He is. He will be who He will be. That is enough for us."

The Pharaoh smiled knowingly. He seemed to have heard it all before. "Ah yes, I see. And this God loves slaves. He likes nothing better than for his slaves to go away for the weekend, and feast and enjoy themselves." He rang the bell for the servant to show them out. "Now listen to me! How dare you treat the Pharaoh as an idiot! The Hebrew slaves can worship whichever God they please, but they must do so in their spare time. You know as well as I do that if I let them go off into the desert for three days, I'll never see them again! Goodbye!"

After they had gone, the Pharaoh called his secretary. "Put out a notice. From now on, the Hebrews must collect all the clay and straw for bricks themselves. We've put up with their little ways long enough. Now they must really be made to work!"

God Gets to Work

"Now look what you've done!" said the Hebrew leaders to Moses and Aaron the following day. "No clay, and no straw for bricks. We have to collect it all ourselves. And yet we must still build at the same rate!"

"I can't help that", said Moses. "We only said what God told us to say. It may be that things have to get worse before they get better."

"But they can't get any worse! We've already lost our only day off", said the Hebrews.

"Well, which do you really want," asked Moses, "a free day or a free life?"

★

Once by himself, Moses knelt and prayed to God. "Living God, why did You ever send me here? Pharaoh won't listen to me, and neither will the Hebrews. We'll never get out of Egypt!"

But God said, "Moses, you must trust Me. By the time I've finished with Pharaoh, he'll be begging you to leave!"

★

Next morning, Moses and Aaron went to wait for Pharaoh. They met him on the way to his daily dip in the River Nile. Moses drew himself to his full height, and Aaron shouted at the top of his voice.

"Great King, you have refused to set the Hebrews free. Now the Living God will show His power!"

With that Aaron struck the river with his stick, and the water began to turn to blood. And so did the streams, the wells, and the puddles, and the baths. There was blood everywhere.

Pharaoh yawned. "Not that old trick again," he said, "my magicians can do the same any day. It's done by stirring up the mud!" So saying, he returned to the Palace. But his magicians couldn't stop him getting thirsty – especially when the blood went on for a week!

★

Well, once God got started, one thing led to another. Without water the fish died, and the whole land began to stink. All the frogs left the rivers and ponds, and went to live in people's houses. Gnats and flies enjoyed the rotting fish, and they began to breed at a terrific rate. They infected the cattle with their bites, and gave everyone boils . . .

From time to time, Moses and Aaron went to see Pharaoh. "The Living God says 'Let My People go!' " But Pharaoh still wouldn't listen. "He has a hard heart, that's his trouble", said Moses, as they came away for the ninth time. "And a stiff neck", said Aaron.

The Last Meal

Egypt was dying. There was no water, and little food. Hailstorms and locusts carried off the crops, and dark clouds covered the sun. Moses called together the Hebrew leaders. "Pack your bags", he said. "Tonight's the night! Now listen carefully . . ."

Following Moses' instructions, every family killed a lamb. They painted some blood on the front door. Then the womenfolk roasted the meat and baked some bread. They cooked without yeast, as there was no time to lose. In any case, the flat bread would pack small and last well.

118

When they were all ready – coats on, sticks handy, animals loaded – they ate their meal. And as they ate, they heard a strange sound outside. The sound of men crying for fear. The sound of women weeping. For that night, Death rode through the land. God punished the Egyptians by killing all their eldest sons. But He passed over the Hebrews, because He saw the blood on their doors.

The Way Out

It was still the early hours of the morning when the message came from Pharaoh: Moses and Aaron were to see him immediately. He was pacing the throne room, sleepless and red-eyed.

"Get out! Get out!" he said, when he saw them. "Take your rabble of slaves and go! And for heaven's sake call off your Living God, before He kills us all!"

Meanwhile, the Egyptians were going down to Goshen with armfuls of clothes and caskets of jewels. "Please take these and leave", they implored. "And say a prayer for us when you get to your land."

*

And so the Hebrews began their new adventure. They didn't know it, but their journey was to last for many years – years of learning the ways of God, ready for living in His Land. They avoided the main coast road. Instead, God led them through scrubland and desert, until they camped by some reed-beds. Ahead of them, the road was water-logged. There was no way forward.

Well, once the Hebrews had gone, the Egyptians began to miss them. There was no one to make bricks, and no one to build cities. No one in fact, to do any of the dirty, dangerous or boring jobs! Pharaoh thought quickly. "Saddle the horses, harness the chariots! We'll catch those Hebrews yet . . ."

A few hours later, the Hebrews saw the Egyptians coming, and despaired. "What have you done now?" they screamed at Moses. "Were the graveyards in Egypt so full that you had to bring us here?"

But Moses was learning. "Trust God", he said quietly. With that, a strong wind began to blow. It swept across the marshes, bowing the reeds, and drying the mud. In no time at all, the people could pick their way to safety. After all the anxiety, it was really quite quick and easy. Away on the horizon, the Egyptians watched with scorn, waiting the order to charge. And then they came, galloping full tilt across the flats, spears levelled, swords raised.

Suddenly, the horses began to stumble. The chariot wheels were sticking. Riders were thrown high in the air, and fell to the ground to be dragged along by reins, or trampled by flashing hooves. The Hebrews turned in unbelieving wonder. The whole of Pharaoh's army, Egypt's pride and joy, was slowly but surely sinking in the mud. Their enemies were disappearing before their very eyes.

In front of them stood Moses, his hands raised in prayer. And as he prayed, the wind ceased, and the water began to seep back. By the time they had returned, there was not a soldier to be seen.

Grumbles

They had been travelling for about six weeks when the food ran out. The little group of ringleaders came to see Moses. "Moses," they said, "we've been thinking about this Living God and this Promised Land, and we've decided we'd like to go home. A Promised Land isn't much good when you've got an empty stomach and a plateful of sand."

Moses looked at them. He knew how they felt, because he was hungry too. "Listen," he said, "if we do nothing else on this journey, we must learn to trust God. He isn't short of food."

But would you believe it? The grumbles went on! At least, they didn't come straight to Moses, but he

124

could hear the muttering, whenever he passed the tents.

"Oh dear," said one, "what would I give for a bowl of Egyptian hot-pot!"

"Yes," said another, "or a nice cool cucumber, or a little pickled fish . . ."

"I know the way this conversation's going", thought Moses. "For two pins they'll vote to go back to slavery, just so they can get their teeth into a nice piece of steak."

And then he heard the quiet voice of God. "Don't worry Moses. This very evening there will be meat in the camp – and plenty of it."

And so it was. At twilight a great flock of birds swooped overhead. The Hebrews watched as they circled round, and then landed for the night. Perhaps hunger had made the Hebrews more alert, or maybe the birds were exhausted. Whichever way it was, the quails were caught, killed, plucked and cooked, before you could say "Bedtime". And no one had dreams of Egyptian hot-pot.

Manna

And sure enough, when they got up the following day, all the bushes were covered with thin, flaky wafers. "This is God's bread", said Moses. "Try it!"

In no time at all, they were fingering the bread and cautiously tasting it. They called it *Manna* which means "What is it?" It was sweet, like honey, and it had to be collected every day, before the sun grew hot and melted it. Moses looked on with delight. They might not live like kings, but at least they would have enough. It seemed that, with God's help, they might just about survive in this weary place.

Water

By now the Hebrews were beginning to enjoy their freedom. Their food tasted better, and even the air smelt fresher. They began to think of themselves not as down-trodden slaves, but as Israelites – the descendants of Jacob who became Israel. The God of Israel was doing something special for them. He was making them into a nation. He was leading them to the Land He had promised.

But there were still problems. Take, for example, the day they camped at Rephidim. It wasn't until all the tents were pitched and the fires lit that they realized there wasn't a drop of water anywhere.

They scanned the horizon for the glint of a lake. They put their ears to the earth for the sound of an underground stream. Nothing! By noon the next day, tempers were getting short. Tongues were dry. Lips were cracked. Children were lying listlessly in the tents, or crying for a drink. The people rounded on Moses.

"Come on, Moses. You got us into this mess. Now you get us out of it. We want water, and we want it now!"

Moses went into his tent to pray. "Living God, what can I do with these people? When will they learn to trust You? Any day now they may put me to death, and scamper back to Egypt."

God answered him. "Moses, take your stick, and a few of the leaders. There's a rock nearby which I will show you. It has been there for centuries, ready for this moment. Water comes down from the hills to this place. When you crack the rock with your stick, water will gush out!"

Moses and the leaders did as God had said. They found the rock, prayed together, and then Moses struck it with his stick. Immediately a trickle of water appeared which quickly became a stream, and then a torrent. The people ran over, calling to each other, and praising God. They plunged their hot faces in the river, and bathed their arms and wrists. They hurried to bring the children – and to fetch the cattle.

Moses was grateful to God. Of course he was. And yet he was sad. He went and sat by himself for a while. It's not easy to be a leader. He had thought it was hard enough with sheep in the wilderness. But people were worse!

130

The Golden Bull

Eventually the Israelites left Rephidim, and came to the slopes of Mount Sinai. This was where God had first spoken to Moses through the burning bush. Somehow it seemed an awesome place. The summit was hidden in clouds of smoke. Now and again they glimpsed a great fire, and felt the earth shake. Moses spoke to the people.

"This is the holy mountain of the Living God. This is where we have come to worship. Wash yourselves, and put on your best clothes."

Two days later, Moses led all the people to the foot of the mountain. Every one of them was trembling with fear. Somewhere, far away, a trumpet was sounding. It came nearer and nearer, louder and louder. And then, when the sense of dread was almost overwhelming, Moses called a halt. He went on alone, higher and higher, until he disappeared.

*

One by one, the people returned to the camp. With Mount Sinai behind them, and with Moses away, they began to talk.

"You know, I don't go along with this idea of an Invisible God. How do we know it's not all cooked up by Moses? Personally, I like a god you can see and touch."

"Right!" said another. "Every other nation has a nice choice of idols. Why should we miss out?"

They went to see Aaron, who had been left in charge.

*

"Aaron, let's face facts. We've seen the last of

Moses. He's disappeared up the mountain, and we haven't seen him for nearly a month. Or must we

believe in an Invisible Moses as well as an Invisible
God?"

Left to himself, Aaron was very weak. God had never wanted him in the first place, remember? Instead of standing up to the people, he joined them. In no time at all, they were bringing their gold bracelets and earrings – the ones the Egyptians had heaped on them when they said goodbye. They threw them into a huge pot, and began to melt them down. Then Aaron got to work. He poured the boiling gold into a great mould. When it had cooled, and the mould was broken away, there stood a dazzling Golden Bull!

Aaron was very pleased with the result. It was the first time he had made an idol, and it had turned out very well. He spoke to the people. "Israelites, this is your God! This is the God who brought us out of Egypt. Bring your sacrifices tomorrow morning, and we'll have a great day of worship and feasting."

The people were so excited that they hardly slept. At last they had a god they could see!

Moses Returns

The following day, as the first rays of the sun began to touch the Golden Bull, the people came with their sacrifices. They prayed and sang and danced all morning. And after that, they all got drunk.

High on the summit of Sinai, God spoke to Moses. "Hurry back to the camp. Your people have thrown Me over in favour of a golden bull. And now they are dancing round it, burning sacrifices."

Moses had been writing God's words on slabs of stone. He carefully lifted them, and set off down the mountainside as fast as he could go. He was ablaze with anger. Before he even came within sight of the camp, he could hear the noise. Raucous drinking songs were ringing across the plain. When he saw the state of the camp, Moses finally lost his temper. God's special people were dancing and fighting, and lurching about, on the very slopes of His holy mountain.

In a rage, Moses lifted the stone slabs high in the air, and smashed them to the ground. The music stopped abruptly. So did the dancing. The people fell silent, stunned at the very sight of Moses.

Without a word, he strode to the Golden Bull, broke it up, melted it, and poured it into a stream. Then he spoke to the people. "Drink it!"

He turned to Aaron. "What in heaven's name made you do such a thing?"

Aaron fell to his knees. "Don't be angry with me, Moses. You know what these people are like, once they get an idea in their heads. They wanted a god they could see. They were prepared to give up their jewels. All I did was melt the gold – and out popped this Bull!"

"And you expect me to believe that?" said Moses. "Don't you see, you've brought death to these people by helping them rebel against God?"

Without waiting for a reply, he strode back towards the mountain. How was he going to explain this to the Living God?

Face to Face

Alone on Mount Sinai, Moses pleaded for the people. He stood between God and Israel, in a final attempt to stop the Lord wiping them out.

God spoke. His voice was like thunder, and the earth shook. "Stand aside, Moses! I have decided to destroy them all. They're no longer worth saving. I'll start again, and make a new nation, beginning with you."

But Moses prayed all the harder. "Living God, remember Your promises! You told Abraham, Isaac and Jacob, that their descendants would have a land of their own. Are You going to break your word? And what will other nations think of the God of Israel?"

At last, God gave way. He promised to allow the Israelites one more chance, and to lead them on into the Promised Land.

And then God said something that Moses had longed to hear. "Moses, you are my friend. I'm closer to you than I am to any other human being. So now I am going to let you see Me. I can't allow you to see My face, because the glory would be too much for you. But hide in a crevice of the rock, and you will see Me pass by."

So Moses sheltered in the rock, and the Living God passed very close to him. But what Moses saw, and how he felt, we shall never know – not in this life, anyway.

God's Way of Life

God now repeated to Moses all that He had said before. And once again, Moses wrote it down carefully on stone slabs. The result was a set of commands by which God wanted His people to live. Some rules seem to spoil life. But these rules were given so that the Israelites would always love God, and treat each other well. When Moses returned to the camp, he read God's Law so that all the people could hear. God says:

1. I am the Lord. I am the one who gave you your freedom. No other god is worth worshipping.
2. Don't worship models, carved images, and idols. Never reduce Me to the size of a doll, and don't try to guess what I look like.
3. Be careful how you use My name. It's not a swear word, and it's not to be taken lightly.

139

4. Keep one day a week as My special day. Enjoy a rest, and make sure everyone else does too.
5. Look up to your father and mother. Families belong together, and must love each other. A happy nation can only be built out of happy families.
6. Always respect the life of others.
7. Always respect marriage, and be loyal to your own partner.
8. Don't steal.
9. Don't tell lies.
10. Don't be jealous of other people. Envy leads on to stealing and murder, so stop it before it starts! God has made you to be yourself, not to spend your time wishing you were someone else.

*

When Moses had finished reading the Ten Commandments, he said: "God had set us free by bringing us out of Egypt. Now He has shown us how to stay free, by keeping His Law. Hands up those who want to live in God's way!"

All the people raised their hands. They solemnly promised to obey God's commands. And God solemnly promised to look after them in return.

Farewell Moses

The years rolled by; forty years, in fact. During that time the Israelites were never far from the Promised Land. But through their own disobedience, they experienced many hardships and suffered many delays.

Moses had sent spies ahead to get some idea of the new land. They brought back tales of fierce giants, which made everyone clamour for Egypt! And so the people turned back to wander round the desert. Slowly and painfully, they learnt to trust God. All those who remembered Egypt died. And the time drew near for Moses to die too. One day he spoke to the people. They were standing on Mount Pisgah.

"Israel, you stand on the threshold of God's Land. Ahead of you lies the fertile valley of the Jordan, with orchards ready-planted and fields ready-ploughed. This is the land that God promised to Abraham, Isaac and Jacob – the land you must now enter."

The people were very hushed and attentive. Somehow they knew what was coming. Moses drew a long breath.

"I say 'You' because I will not be coming. Joshua has been my second-in-command these many years. He will be your new leader."

With that, Moses blessed them, and walked away.

They never found his body. He had simply gone to be with God.

143

Gideon

Joash lived in the village of Ophrah. He was a proud man – proud to be alive, proud to be a Jew, proud to have a son. His son's name was Gideon.

Whenever they walked out together, Joash would tell Gideon the story of the old days, the days of Moses, the days of Joshua. He showed his son the twelve standing stones on the bank of the Jordan.

"That's the very spot where Joshua crossed the river", he said. "The Living God held back the waters, and they crossed on dry land. Ah!" he said, "those were the days!"

On another occasion, Joash showed Gideon the ruins of Jericho. "That was the greatest conquest Joshua ever made – and without so much as a siege gun", he said. "The people simply marched round the walls every day for a week, and then gave a great shout – and blew the rams' horns."

"And what happened then, Father?" said Gideon, as if he hadn't heard the story a hundred times before. "Why, my son, the walls simply collapsed!" He flicked his fingers, "Just like that! The Living God gave them the city!"

"Whatever became of the Living God?" said Gideon to his father one day. Joash looked very thoughtful, and very sad. "Whatever became of the people of God?" he said, as if that was a reply.

The truth was that the Israelites had fallen on hard times. They had no real leaders, and were under constant attack from their neighbours, the Midianites. Raiding parties would come at any time of the day or night, firing the crops and stealing the cattle. Life was so impossible, that many Israelites had taken to living in caves in the hills. It was a far cry from the days of Joshua.

To make matters worse, they had begun to worship idols again. Wherever you looked, on hilltops, or under green trees, or in fields of corn, there were statues and altars to the gods of Baal. Even Joash had an altar – just for luck.

★

One day, when Gideon was a young man, the
Living God spoke to him. "Gideon, take a pair of
bulls, and tear down your father's pagan altar. Build
a new altar, and offer a sacrifice to Me."

That night, Gideon obeyed God. He demolished the altar of Baal, and built an altar to the Living God. He chopped up a pole belonging to the goddess Asherah, and used it for fire-wood. Then he offered a seven-year-old bull to the Lord.

The following day, the whole village was up in arms. They wanted to stone Gideon for destroying the altar of Baal. But Joash spoke up for his son. "I'm sure there's no need for you to take revenge," he said, "Baal and Asherah can stand up for themselves." He winked at Gideon. "Or can they?"

Gideon's Army

After that, Gideon prayed to God.

"Living Lord, I'm not proud like my father. I'm not a very important men. Nor is my family. Nor is my tribe. So why are you calling on me to destroy the altars and attack the Midianites?"

"Because when you admit you are weak, you have to let Me do the fighting", said God.

But Gideon was still not sure, so he asked the Lord for a sign. "Living God, I will lay some wool on the ground tonight. If, in the morning, there's dew on the wool, but not on the ground, I'll know that You are with me."

Well, the next morning there was so much dew on the wool, that Gideon could almost fill a bucket. And yet the ground was as dry as a bone. And, just to make doubly sure, the Lord worked the miracle again the following night. This time the wool was dry and the ground was wet. Gideon was convinced. "Living God, You *are* calling me to save Israel. So be it."

No sooner had Gideon told people what he would do, than thirty-two thousand men came to join him. But God said, "Remember, it's weakness that I use. You can send them all home, except for three hundred."

Gideon did so. Then he and his tiny army hid in the hills, and kept watch on the Midianite camp. Spread out below them, the enemy looked like a swarm of locusts. Under cover of darkness, Gideon and two friends slipped past the Midianite guards. They went to listen in on the talk in the tents.

"I had a terrible dream last night," said someone, "I saw a loaf of barley roll into our camp and flatten a tent!"

"Well, the meaning of that's plain enough!" said another. "That loaf was Gideon and that tent was us! I don't like it at all . . ."

Outside, Gideon breathed a prayer of thanks. "Living God, these Midianites are beaten before they start!"

Back at the camp, Gideon divided his men into three groups. He gave everyone a jar, with a torch inside it – and a trumpet! Just before midnight, they surrounded the Midianite camp. Then, at a signal from Gideon, they blew the trumpets – and smashed the jars. Holding high their torches, they shouted, "For God and for Gideon!"

Well, that was all the Midianites needed! They had been frightened enough, without the unnerving sound of three hundred jars being broken to smithereens. Scrambling blindly from their tents, they saw the flames leaping down the hillside. In their army, only officers carried torches, and each officer had ten men. To their eyes, they were surrounded by at least three thousand!

Without more ado, the Midianites drew their
swords, and started fighting each other in the dark.
And all the time the voices drew nearer, crying "For

God and for Gideon! For God and for Gideon!" At last, terror overwhelmed them. The Midianites threw down their weapons, and fled.

151

Saul

The Israelites, or Jews as they were now called,
continued to live in the Promised Land. They had
constant battles with their neighbours – first the
Midianites, then the Amalekites, and then the
Philistines. From time to time, God gave them a
great leader, like Gideon, or a great prophet, like
Samuel. But there was never anyone as great as
Moses. How they missed him!

People still found it hard to believe in the
Invisible God. All the other nations had gods you
could see – and kings too. The Jews simply longed
for a king! Of course, they knew that the Living
God was their King, but somehow that wasn't
enough . . .

And that brings us to Saul. Or at least, it brings us
to the donkeys! Saul's father, a wealthy man by the
name of Kish, had lost his donkeys. Quite how they
got away we shall never know. But by the time Saul
was sent to fetch them, they had wandered many
miles. Saul and his servant tracked them for three
days, over hills and through valleys, but without
success.

"It's no good," said Saul at last, "we've lost them
and that's that. If we don't turn for home, Father
will think he's lost us as well."

But the servant had an idea. "There's a holy man who lives not far from here, the prophet Samuel. They say he knows all secrets, so let's go and ask him where the donkeys are!"

And that was how Saul met Samuel. Samuel was a "see-er", someone who could see the secrets of men's hearts. Someone who could see into the mind of God Himself. Not surprisingly, with such a gift, he already knew that Saul was coming!

On the previous day, God had said to Samuel, "I know the people want a king they can see – a captain to lead the fight against the Philistines, a judge to give justice and get things organized. So tomorrow I will send you Saul. He comes from a small family in the smallest tribe, but he's a head taller than most people, and very handsome. He is My choice for King."

So when Saul arrived, it seemed no time to discuss donkeys. "Never mind about them," said Samuel, "they've been found long ago. They were just God's way of bringing you here. Now come and sit down."

Samuel had invited all the local leaders to a dinner. They were there to offer special sacrifices, and many of them would have liked to be king. But Samuel sat Saul at the head of the table, and gave him the best slices of meat. All day they feasted and, when evening came, Saul was given a place to sleep on one of the flat roofs.

The following morning, Samuel strolled out of town with Saul to see him on his way. But before they parted, he produced a flask of olive oil. He told Samuel to kneel down, and poured the oil all over his head!

"This is the sign of God's blessing poured out upon you", he said. "You are to be King of Israel. You must protect the people from themselves and from their enemies. And to prove that what I say is true, as soon as you leave here, two men will tell you where your donkeys are!"

So Saul got up and went his way. He met the men, and he found the donkeys. But by then he had other things on his mind!

154

A King at Last!

Not long after that, Samuel summoned the people to meet him on the broad plain of Mizpah. He stood up and delivered one of his greatest speeches. When Samuel spoke, it was like hearing the voice of God. After all, that's what prophets are for.

"The Living God brought you out of Egypt", he cried. "He brought you through the reeds and across the wilderness. He made sure you captured the Land, and helped you to beat your enemies . . ."

"Oh yes, we know all that", said some of his hearers. "Why don't you come to the point?"

"The point is," said Samuel, "the point is that you keep nagging for a king. The Living God is your king, but that doesn't seem to satisfy you. You clamour at me for a real one! So this is it. Today God lets you have your wish. Today we choose a king!"

One by one, the tribes marched forward, to see if God was choosing a king from among them. First the largest and most important, but Samuel waved them on. Then the medium-sized tribes – Samuel dismissed them too. Finally, the little tribe of Benjamin. Everyone thought there was some mistake, but Samuel raised his hand for silence.

"This is the Royal Tribe!" Samuel walked slowly along the ranks. He was an old man, with shaggy eyebrows, leaning on a stick. He peered closely into each face. At last he came to the end.

"God's man is not here", he said. There was a snigger from the larger tribes. "The old fool doesn't know what he's doing half the time!"

But Samuel spoke up. "I see where he is! His name is Saul, and he's over there!"

Sure enough, there was Saul, huddling his great height beneath a waggon, and pretending to change a wheel. They brought him out. Samuel presented him to the people.

"Children of Israel, this is your king! He comes from a small family in a small tribe. But he's a head taller than most men, and very handsome. He's the best we have!" The people were rather surprised at the choice, but somehow they managed to cheer. "Long live the King!"

Sometimes God gives us what we want, because we insist. But it's not always for the best!

*

At first, Saul continued to work on his farm. Not having had a king before, there was no palace, no crown, and no robes. So Saul carried on much as before. And then, after about a month, came his first test.

156

The King of Ammon was threatening the town of Jabesh. He said that if the people didn't surrender, he would capture them and take out their eyes. He gave them a week to think it over. The leaders of Jabesh were desperate. Then they said "Wait! We have a king now. This is a problem for him."

They sent a message to Saul, who was ploughing a field at the time. He immediately called on every fighting man to join him. Then he said to the messengers, "Tell Jabesh we'll be there tomorrow!"

At dawn the following day, Saul attacked the Ammonites with the united armies of Israel. By noon they had slaughtered most, and scattered the rest. The Jews were overjoyed.

"Now we know that Saul is God's King!" they cried. They carried him in triumph to Gilgal, where they gave him a proper coronation, and a fine feast to mark the day.

The Big Mistake

After that, Saul waged many successful campaigns. Under his leadership, the people gained in confidence and self-respect. One day Samuel came to see him.

"King Saul," he said, "remember that I was the one who anointed you. Now listen to what God says."

"I am listening", said Saul.

"God has work for you to do", said Samuel solemnly. "He wants you to wipe out the Amalekites. They are a boastful and wicked people. They have opposed God's plans ever since our folk came out of Egypt. Now they can no longer be allowed to survive. They must be destroyed, from greatest king to tiniest baby, and their cattle and belongings as well."

"If God wants it, so be it", said Saul.

In the weeks that followed, Saul routed the armies of Amalek. He chased them to the very borders of Egypt, killing the people and burning their towns. But when he saw the sheep and cattle, camels and donkeys, he thought it a waste to slaughter them. And there were a lot of nice things in the palaces and homes, which it seemed a pity to destroy. So Saul let his soldiers keep them. Worst of all, when the King of Amalek himself was captured, Saul decided to spare his life. "He's useless without his army," he thought, "and it will look good to have a king grovelling under my table. I'll cut off his thumbs and feed him on scraps."

★

And then Samuel called on Saul again. The king welcomed him with a grin.

"Welcome, honoured prophet!" he said. "You heard about the Amalekites? You see, I'm always ready to help the Living God!"

But Samuel's brow was as dark as thunder. "Is that so?" he said. "Then perhaps you can explain all the mooing and bleating. You seem to have a lot more livestock than when I saw you last."

Saul thought quickly. "Ah, that wasn't me, that was my men. They decided to keep the best of the cattle when we defeated Amalek. Only to bring back as sacrifices, of course! We killed everything else, just as you said . . ."

"Sacrifices, sacrifices!" stormed Samuel. "What does the Living God care about sacrifices? He looks for obedience! You were told to wipe out Amalek, from greatest king to tiniest baby, and their cattle and belongings as well, and you haven't done it! You've kept treasure, ornaments, furniture, live-stock – in fact everything you fancied. You've even spared the king!"

Saul hung his head. "I had to do it, Samuel. I was afraid of my men, and did what they wanted."

"And now God wishes He had never chosen you as King", said the prophet. "From now on, you're on your own. Goodbye!"

Samuel turned to leave, but Saul grabbed him.

159

"Samuel, stay with me! I can't rule without you!"
But Samuel tore himself away, leaving part of his
cloak in Saul's hands. He strode out of the king's
presence without pausing to bow, and was never
seen there again.

Goliath

Israel was in deep trouble. The Philistines were on the march, and this time they had a champion to defeat all comers. His name was Goliath of Gath. He stood three metres high, and was dressed in bronze from head to foot. Every day he would stride out and jeer at the Israelites.

"Good morning, little people, this is Goliath speaking!" he bellowed. "Why don't you send someone to fight me? Don't try to tell me you're scared!" He brandished his great spear, so that the Jewish soldiers broke ranks and ran for cover. Then he turned and went back to his camp with a great laugh. This went on morning and evening, for more than a month.

One day, the Israelites had a visitor. A boy called David came from Bethlehem, bringing food for his brothers. He wasn't in the army himself, because he was too young. He stayed at home, looking after his father's sheep. David was surprised to find everyone so gloomy. Even King Saul sat staring into space.

162

"But you are the army of the Living God", he said to anyone who would listen. "You needn't be scared of a Philistine, even if he *is* a giant! Anyway," he added, "he's a sitting duck for a catapult!" He went to see the King.

"Your Majesty," he said, "I'm not afraid of Goliath of Gath. I've killed lions and bears in my work as a shepherd. If God has kept me safe then, I'm sure He will help me now."

Saul was the only man with any armour, and he readily offered it to David. Mind you, Saul was taller than anyone else, and David was only a lad, so the result was quite ridiculous. The helmet came down over his eyes, and the sword trailed along the ground.

"It's no good," said David, "I must stick to what I know." He took the catapult from his belt, picked five smooth stones from the stream, and went out to meet Goliath.

The giant of Gath was just beginning his usual speech. "Good evening, little people, this is Goliath

speaking . . ." Suddenly a movement caught his eye. A young boy was walking towards him from the ranks of the Israelites. He made a few swatting movements with his great sword. "Run along, sonny. If you hang around here, you could get hurt!"

"And so could you!" cried David, fingering one of the five smooth stones. "You may be covered in brass from head to foot, but I come to fight you in the name of the Living God!" With that, he sent the stone singing through the air, and hit Goliath right between the eyes!

With a look of utter surprise, the giant rocked back on his heels, and then crashed forward on his face. He rolled over and lay still. Quick as a flash, David ran up, seized his enemy's sword, and cut off his head.

Jealousy

Young David became a hero overnight. Saul made him an officer in the army, and refused to hear of him going back home. Jonathan, Saul's son, swore undying friendship, and gave David his suit of armour. Only royalty had armour at that time, as there was a shortage of blacksmiths in Israel. It was really quite a compliment, and not at all a bad fit.

In every town, people turned out to sing the praises of Saul and David. Now and again, they could hear the words: "Saul has killed thousands, but David tens of thousands!" The king took it well at first, but after a while he became sullen. Saul decided to keep a close watch on David. If old Samuel got hold of him, he'd certainly make him king. So Saul kept him at the palace, and asked him to play the harp.

As the days went by, Saul suffered more and more from black moods. On one occasion, he even snatched up a spear and tried to pin David to the wall. It was clear to both of them that Saul was insanely jealous. The God who had rejected one king was now choosing another.

Saul began sending David out to fight the Philistines, hoping he would get himself killed. But no such thing happened. Rather, David returned covered in glory, and married the king's daughter.

One evening, Jonathan walked with David to the Palace gate.

"David, I'll be frank with you. My father is planning to have you killed. You must run for your life. But believe me, whatever happens, we will stick together."

They gave each other a farewell hug, and David left to join Samuel at Ramah.

Jonathan

When Saul heard that David had escaped, he stormed up and down the Palace in a rage.

"Jonathan," he said, "you're a fool! Don't you realize that as long as David lives, you can never be king?" But that was the last thing on Jonathan's mind. He kept in touch with David by secret signs and messages, so that David would know it was unsafe to return.

*

Once David was on the run, he was joined by dozens of supporters. Soon he had a small army of his own. They went into hiding east of Wild Goat Rock.

Saul decided to grasp the nettle. His crown wasn't safe while David was free. The young man must be hunted down and stopped. As chance would have it, the search led to the very cave where David was hiding. Saul went in and sat in the shade for a while, not guessing that David was tip-toeing up behind him with a knife. However, instead of stabbing Saul as anyone else might have done, David carefully cut off a piece of his coat. Then he crept back the way he had come.

Just as Saul was leaving, David called to him from a nearby cliff. "Have you forgotten something, My Lord?" he asked, waving the piece of cloth. "You ought to be more careful where you sit in future!"

With an effort, Saul managed to control himself. "Is that you David, dear boy?" he said. "We just happened to be passing."

"You just happen to be hunting me!" said David. "Don't you see, I wish you no harm? I could have killed you just now, but you are God's chosen king. Woe betide anyone who harms a hair of your head!"

Saul burst into great shuddering sobs. The cares of leadership had worn him down. In any case, he was a sick man. "You're a better man than I am, David," he cried, "I'm not fit to be your king."

*

One day, Saul was fighting the Philistines on
Mount Gilboa. The battle went against Israel, and
they had to run for their lives. Saul was hit by
enemy arrows, and badly wounded. His three sons,
including Jonathan, had already been killed. Now
he fell on his sword, rather than be taken alive.
When David heard the news, he tore his clothes in
grief, and sprinkled earth on his head. Later, he
wrote this song:

> Saul and Jonathan, heroes both;
> Together in life, together in death.

Bathsheba

With Saul dead, it was only a matter of time before David became king. He chose Jerusalem as his capital, and set about turning it into a fine city. In due course, he began to wonder about building a Temple. "After all," he said, "here I sit in my fine palace. Why shouldn't the Living God have a House as well?"

*

Some years later, David decided to leave the fighting to his generals. He sent out Joab with the Israelite army, while he himself remained in Jerusalem. He was middle-aged. He was tired of war. He needed to relax . . .

Late one afternoon, he was walking in the roof garden, when he caught sight of a young woman. She was taking a bath, quite unaware that the king was watching her! David summoned a servant. "Find out who lives in that house down there, would you?" he said. "I can tell you that myself, Sir," said the servant, "her name is Bathsheba. She's married to a professional soldier by the name of Uriah." He looked knowingly at the king. "They say she gets lonely."

"Not any more", said David. "Tell her I'd like her to come round as soon as possible."

That night Bathsheba came to the palace. She was the most beautiful woman David had ever seen, and they became lovers. "I know she's another man's wife," David told himself, "but that man is one of my soldiers, so she comes under my command as well."

Before long, Bathsheba became pregnant. David realized he had a scandal on his hands, so he sent a letter to Joab. "Dear Commander, you have a man in your company named Uriah. I want him put in the front line where the battle is fierce and the fighting heavy." Joab did so, and Uriah was killed. When Bathsheba heard of her husband's death, she wept for him. Then she moved into the palace to live with David. The king was pleased with himself. In the space of a few days, he had stolen a wife and murdered a husband. There was life in the old dog yet!

But God was not pleased. Not pleased at all!

171

Discovered!

David and Bathsheba were the talk of the town. People were amazed that she had got over her husband's death so quickly. But one man was not impressed. His name was Nathan. He was a prophet.

Nathan asked to see the King. "Come in", said David. "And what can I do for you?"

"I want to tell you a story", said Nathan.

"Go ahead," said David, "my time is yours."

"Once upon a time there were two men," said Nathan, "one was immensely rich, and the other was very poor. The rich man had cattle and sheep to cover a hundred hills. The poor man had just one

ewe lamb, which he reared in his own house as a pet. He fed it from his own plate, watered it from his own cup, and nursed it in his own lap."

"Very moving", said David, wondering how to get rid of him. Prophets can be a terrible bore. But Nathan went on. "One day a visitor arrived at the rich man's house. The rich man didn't want to kill one of his own animals, so he went and took the poor man's only ewe lamb, and cooked that instead."

Suddenly, David was listening. That sort of thing made him furious. Why, it was his job as king to put a stop to this sort of bullying. He thumped the table. "By the Living God!" he said. "Tell me where this rich man lives. I'll make him pay if it's the last thing I do!"

"He lives here", said Nathan quietly. "You are the man. After all God has done for you, you have killed Uriah and taken his wife. Yes you, who have wives to spare!"

David sank into a chair, his head in his hands. It was all too true.

173

"I have sinned against the Lord", he said. "How can He ever forgive me?"

"The Lord will always forgive those who are sorry," said Nathan, "but there is a price to be paid. Bathsheba's baby will die."

For days, David refused to eat anything. Every night he locked himself in his room, and lay on the floor in prayer.

"Lord, I'm sorry. But please, Lord, spare the child!"

A week later, the baby died. For a while, no one dared to tell the king, but he guessed it from their faces.

"Is the child dead?" he asked.

"Yes, he is", they replied.

After that, David and Bathsheba became more settled. They had done wrong, and they had paid for it. They grew to love each other very much, and in due course God gave them another son. They called him Solomon.

Absalom

David was growing old. Among his sons was a young man called Absalom. They said he was the best-looking prince in Israel – and he knew it! His hair was long, his manners were charming, and his father doted on him. But Absalom was not to be trusted. When Joab was so bold as to disagree with him, he found his farm "accidentally" burnt down. And a brother who offended him was murdered at a party – Absalom's party.

There was no doubt about it, Absalom wanted to be king. He started to curry favour with the visitors to Jerusalem. He sat at the city gate, asking people their business. "You're on your way to court? Oh, how I wish I could help you!" he would say.

175

"There's no justice to be had in Israel these days." And then, as if struck by a sudden thought, he would add, "Now if I were in charge..." Naturally, folk were delighted to have a prince who was so interested in their problems. Just by sitting at the gate for four years, Absalom won friends for himself all over the country.

And then, one day, he made his move. He sent signals to all his supporters to take over their towns, blow the trumpets, and shout "Absalom is King!"

The coup went according to plan. Absalom was proclaimed king at Hebron, and began to march on Jerusalem. Rather than fight his own son, David decided to leave the city.

It was a sad day. The inhabitants of Jerusalem wept to see the king going, with all his family and officials – and six hundred soldiers who had served him in the old days.

When he reached the slopes of the Mount of Olives, David turned and looked back. Spread out below him was Jerusalem, God's city. The first capital of Israel. He wept.

Joab

As David departed, Absalom arrived. He rode proudly in his chariot, his long hair blowing behind him. And with him marched a mighty army.

Ahithophel, one of David's wise advisers, went straight over to Absalom's side. Joab, on the other hand, refused to leave David. Hushai also wanted to go with David, but the King asked him to stay behind. "Pretend you have deserted me," he said, "and do your best to confuse Absalom's council."

There followed an interesting meeting. Ahithophel was all for chasing David straight away. "Give me twelve thousand men tonight, and we'll catch him while he's cold." But Hushai gave different advice. "With all due respect to Ahithophel," he said, "I think on this occasion he's

wrong. David is an old hand at guerrilla warfare. No one catches him once he's in the hills. And remember, he has all the Old Guard with him, six hundred of the hardest fighters in Israel!"

Absalom winced. "So what do you suggest?" he said to Hushai.

"Let's get the country united behind you, My Lord. Then, with such massive support, you should have no trouble in flushing out the Old Man." In the ensuing murmurs of agreement, Ahithophel stormed out of the room.

Meanwhile, David had gathered an army. He divided his troops into three parties, and gave them clear orders: "On no account must any of you harm Absalom." Then they fought the battle of their lives in the forest of Ephraim. Twenty thousand

178

Israelites were killed that day, and even more got lost in the wooded countryside. Absalom himself, who was no soldier, got caught by his hair in a tree. He was still hanging there helpless when Joab found him. Ignoring David's orders, Joab speared Absalom to death.

Back at the city of Mahanaim, David awaited news of the fighting. At last a soldier came running, and fell exhausted at the king's feet. "The battle is won, My Lord!" he cried.

"And Absalom? What about Absalom?" asked David. But the messenger wouldn't reply. His silence said it all. Broken-hearted, David went to his room. Throwing himself onto the bed, he said over and over again: "Absalom, Oh Absalom my son. If only I could have died instead of you!"

Joab arrived and went in to plead with him. "My Lord, your army is creeping home as if it was afraid to win battles. These men have just saved your life, to say nothing of the lives of your family. Did you really want Absalom alive and well, and all the rest of us dead?"

"All right, Joab," sighed David, "I take your point. Let the celebrations commence!"

Soon there was music and dancing in the streets of Mahanaim, and the parties went on until the early hours. But through it all, David stood leaning over the battlements, staring into space. And silently the tears ran down his cheeks.

Solomon

King David had reigned for forty years. He had started as a shepherd, made his name as a soldier, and won his people's hearts as king. No one ever cared for ordinary folk more than David. Under his leadership, Israel was united for the first and last time. All the land promised to Abraham was brought under a single rule.

Now David was old. With Bathsheba at his side, he called Solomon to see him. "Solomon," he said, "you must be king after me."

"If you wish it, Father", said Solomon.

"Be brave my son", said David. "Follow the Law of Moses, and do whatever God tells you to do." He smiled: "That way, you won't go far wrong."

A few days later, David died. In spite of all his achievements, he had never succeeded in building the Temple. But he had gathered all the materials together, ready for Solomon to do the work.

★

One night, the Living God spoke to Solomon. "What would you like me to do for you?" he said to the young king. Solomon thought hard.

"Living God, give me the wisdom I need to rule your people. Guide me in my decisions. Help me know right from wrong."

The Lord was pleased. "You could have asked for long life, or riches, or for your enemies to drop dead", He said. "But you have made a good choice. I will give you more wisdom and understanding than anyone has ever had before or will ever have again. And you can have long life and riches to go with it."

And so it was. Wherever Solomon's name is known, men speak of his wisdom, even today.

King Ahab

Solomon reigned for forty years. He built a wonderful Temple in Jerusalem, and his wealth and wisdom became a legend. After him, however, the Jews drifted into trouble again. There was a succession of kings who cared little for the Living God. In the end the nation was torn in two, to make Israel in the north and Judah in the south. Each part had its own king.

One of the strongest kings of the north was Ahab. He was also one of the worst. His great mistake was to marry a princess from Tyre. Her name was Jezebel, and she brought her gods and goddesses with her. She soon had Ahab building a temple to Baal in Samaria.

But the Living God didn't leave Himself without a voice. On the contrary, the greatest man of God since Moses emerged to stand up to Ahab. His name was Elijah, and he was a prophet.

The gods of Baal were gods of nature. They were worshipped to make sure that the crops grew and that women had children. It was understandable that pagan tribes should worry about such things. But the stories of those gods were terrible – full of lust and blood. Nothing could be further from the love and patience of the Living God.

The more these gods were worshipped in Israel, the more angry Elijah became. Finally, he strode into Ahab's Palace, and spoke God's mind. It was time to show which God was true:

"In the name of the Living God of Israel, whom I serve, there will be no dew or rain for the next two or three years, until I say so. See what your Baal makes of that!"

Having said that, Elijah stalked out. Ahab sat back on his throne, feeling dizzy with shock. These wild prophets who sprang in from nowhere could be very frightening. But Queen Jezebel was made of sterner stuff.

"Are you the King around here or not?" she said. "That man needs his head cutting off. And anyone else who trusts in the God of Israel should be thrown into prison!"

"Yes, yes dear, I'm sure you're absolutely right", said Ahab. "I'll see to it straight away."

But try as they would, Ahab's servants could not find Elijah anywhere. He seemed to have vanished from the face of the earth. In actual fact, God had sent Elijah east of Jordan, to the brook Cherith. There he would be safe from the king's anger, and have a steady supply of water. As for food, God sent ravens with bread, meat, and fruit.

And so the great drought began.

Contest on Carmel

For almost three years there was no rain in Israel –
not a drop. The harvests failed in the parched
ground. Animals died – and so did people.

"That man Elijah must be brought to me", said
King Ahab. "He threatened me with this drought.
It's all his fault."

Elijah appeared from his desert hiding-place, and
stood before Ahab and Jezebel. "So!" said the
King, "Enter Israel's greatest troublemaker!"

"It takes one to know one!" replied Elijah. "It's
not me who troubles Israel. It's you, your queen,
and those thugs you call Prophets of Baal! Bring
your supporters to Mount Carmel, and we'll see
what your gods can do."

"Very well," said Ahab, "I agree!"

So Ahab summoned all the Israelites, and the
nine hundred Prophets of Baal, to meet at Mount
Carmel. They built two altars, one to Baal and one
to the Living God. On each altar they heaped

firewood, and then laid meat on top ready for the sacrifices.

"Remember," said Elijah, "we're not setting fire to the wood. It's up to our gods to provide the flame. That shouldn't prove too difficult."

Straight away the Prophets of Baal began to pray. They screamed and shouted, whirled and danced. They fell flat on their faces, and cut themselves with knives. This went on for several hours, until they were exhausted and lame. But nothing happened.

Elijah cheered them on. "Come on, lads!" he cried. "You can do it! Pray louder! Maybe Baal is deaf, or taking a nap? I know! He's gone to the bathroom!"

In the middle of the afternoon, the Prophets of Baal gave up. They knew they were beaten. And then Elijah grew very serious. He called the people to gather round. Together they built an altar of twelve round stones, one for every tribe of Israel. Then Elijah placed wood on it, and laid his sacrifice on top. Not content with that, he dug a trench all round the altar.

"Fetch plenty of water", he said. "Pour it over the wood and over the sacrifice, until it fills the trench. I want you to be sure there's no cheating." It was hard work bringing the water, and it seemed a wicked waste after all the drought, but the people did so.

"Now let us pray together", said Elijah. "O Lord, God of Abraham, Isaac, and Jacob, prove now that you are the God of Israel and that I am your servant. Send fire from heaven, that this people may know that you are the Living God!"

There was a pause. Elijah stood with his hands

raised to heaven. The nine hundred Prophets of Baal sat nursing their feet, and staunching their wounds. The people waited.

And then the fire fell. Great flames consumed the wood, burnt the meat, and licked up the water in the trench. Even the stones crumbled and cracked, and the earth all around was scorched. When the people saw it, they fell to the ground.

"The God of Israel, He is God!" they cried. "He alone is God!"

"Seize the Prophets of Baal!" said Elijah. "Let none of them escape." They seized them.

While the people ate, Elijah went to the top of Mount Carmel, and prayed for rain. Deep in his bones, he knew the drought was going to end. Sure enough, far away on the horizon, appeared a cloud. It was about the size of a fist. Then came another. And then another . . . Elijah sent a message to Ahab.

"Get in your chariot, and head for home!" But it was too late. The rain was already falling in heavy drops. It was a hard day for Ahab – caught by fire and water in the same afternoon!

188

Horeb

When Jezebel heard the news, her anger was terrible. She made a solemn vow: "May the gods strike me dead if I don't have Elijah's life by this time tomorrow!"

So once more Elijah had to flee. He ran and walked in the wilderness for a whole day, until he could go no further. At last he lay down under a tree. All he wanted to do was die. "Living God, I'm still the only man in Israel who really believes in You. The rest will soon go back to Baal. I can't go on any longer. Please let me perish!" Exhausted, he fell asleep.

He awoke to find a loaf of bread and a jug of water by his side. "Someone must care for me", he thought, looking round. "Perhaps there are folk in these parts who still love the Living God, and take pity on a prophet." He ate and drank, and slept again. The next time he woke he felt better. He decided to go to Mount Horeb – the place where Moses met the Lord. It would take a month to get there, but that was where he wanted to be.

At Horeb, the Lord God spoke to Elijah. "What are you doing here?" He said. "It's more than my life is worth to stay in Israel," said Elijah, "I'm the only one of your prophets left, and Jezebel has sworn to have my head."

Suddenly a great gale began to blow. Wind roared through the gullies, tearing pieces of rock from the very mountainside, and sending boulders crashing down the slopes. Just as suddenly the wind ceased, and an earthquake made the landscape shudder and leap. Tongues of flame sprang from

cracks and crevices, so that the whole place seemed alight.

And then, in the ensuing stillness, God spoke. His voice was a mere whisper. "Elijah, I am with you. I have many things for you to do. Don't be afraid. By the time I've finished, there will be seven thousand people in Israel who will be loyal to Me and Me alone. Now go back to your work!"

190

Amos

At long last, Israel prospered. The farmers produced more fruit, grain and meat than they needed, and merchants began to trade with other countries. However, as often happens, the smaller farmers began to suffer. They had very little surplus to sell, and were given precious little for it. Some had to sell their land, and became slaves. At the same time, the people of the Northern Kingdom were very religious. Three times a year they held pilgrimages to the shrines at Beersheba, Bethel and Gilgal. They came from far and wide to offer sacrifices, and to let God know how well they were doing.

One day, a new prophet arrived in the North. His name was Amos. He walked through the streets and markets of Bethel, looking at the wealth of clothes and jewellery, and sizing up the price of the houses. As he passed the gardens and verandahs, he could hear the ladies taking tea. ("Oh, do pour me another!" "Well, I could just manage the teeniest slice more!")

Amos wasn't a prophet by birth or calling. He was in fact a herdsman from Tekoah in Judah. But God had a bone to pick with the people of Israel, and he had sent Amos to do the picking.

"Listen, people of Israel! Your way of life is one big lie! You make all these pilgrimages to worship God, but you don't obey His Law. Look at your shoes! Did you pay a fair price for them? That blanket you carry, was it taken from someone who needed it? Your clothes were made by someone who had hardly enough to eat; but you didn't care. You

191

barge through life without a thought for your duty
to others."

Naturally, people tried to silence him. "Hold
your tongue!" they said. "You don't come from
these parts, so what do you know about it?"

"My information comes from the Living God",
said Amos. "I speak because He tells me to. If a lion
roars, aren't you afraid? If God speaks, shouldn't
you listen?"

Suddenly the crowd parted to make way for
Amaziah. He was the priest in Bethel, and he was
doing very nicely from the pilgrim traffic.

"That's quite enough from you, young man. I'm
sure the people back home would like to hear your
prophecies, so why don't you run along?"

But Amos stood his ground. "I'm not a prophet, sir", he said. "At least, I'm not a professional. I'm a mere shepherd from Tekoah. But the Living God has given me a message, so how can I be silent? The Lord's judgement is about to fall on Israel, Amaziah. Your own children will be killed, and you yourself will be carried off into Exile. You mark my words!"

Hosea

Another prophet who worked in the north, was Hosea. The great agony in his life was that his marriage was in ruins. God had told him to marry a woman called Gomer. She wasn't quite the sort Hosea would have chosen. She was a shocking flirt and wore far too much make-up. But Hosea did as he was told, and married her all the same.

Well, their life was a misery. Gomer spent all her time in front of the mirror, admiring herself and dreaming of boyfriends. She had one affaire after another. "Everyone does it," she explained to Hosea, "and anyway, what do you think you are, the Law of Moses?"

Hosea became the laughing-stock of the whole town. Whoever heard of a man like him in love with a girl like her? They were as different as chalk from cheese. And then, one day, it all made sense to Hosea. "Why!" he said to himself, "when Gomer lets me down and runs off with other men, I feel absolutely wretched. And that's how God must feel

when Israel runs after other gods!"

He went in search of Gomer. "Darling, let's start again . . ."

*

Later, Hosea spoke to the people:

"Hear what the Living God says! You are my people and I love you. My heart will never let you go. Stop playing around with idols who can neither save nor help. Come back with Me to the desert days, and be poor once more. There I will win your hearts again, and life can start afresh."

Isaiah

Far away to the north, a great new empire had grown up. Her name was Assyria. To the wider world, Israel and Judah were nothing but tiny buffer states, wedged between super-powers. Ahaz, the King of Judah, was a frightened man. This was no time for a little country to be independent. He needed help, but he didn't know which way to turn. Desperately, he strengthened the walls of Jerusalem, and kept his fingers crossed.

But among the King's counsellors was a prophet named Isaiah. As a young man, Isaiah had been given a glimpse of God that no one could ever forget. Now he knew that the Lord must punish both Israel and Judah. But he also believed that God would not forget them. He even called his son "Shear Jasub", which means "A few will come back". Isaiah went to see the king. He found him looking at the battlements and anxiously biting his nails.

"Oh, Isaiah, I'm glad you've come", said the King. "Tell me what you think of the work so far. We're making the walls twelve feet thick, and a good deal higher. We're also putting more arrow slits in the towers . . ."

Very gently, Isaiah interrupted. "My Lord, we serve the Living God. Let's put our trust in Him. There's no need to fret and fuss when He's on our side."

"No, I suppose you're right", said the King, trying not to sound confused. ("Fancy Isaiah dragging God into it!" he said to himself).

★

In due course, the Northern Kingdom of Israel fell to the Assyrian army. Amos and Hosea had said something like that would happen, and it did. The king was killed, and the entire population was carried off. They were never seen again. The Southern Kingdom had no choice but to surrender. It was a dark day for the Jews.

But Isaiah saw things God's way, and he gave them a message of hope:

"The tree of David has been cut down.
But listen! One day a new shoot will grow
from this old stump.
A King will come who will give us Peace,
    Peace that will spread,
    Peace that will last.
Then tears will be dried and crying will stop,
The tramp of boots will fade away,
And swords will turn to hoes.
Wolves and sheep will live together,
And the bear will look for clover
with the cow."

The Siege

In due course, a king named Hezekiah succeeded Ahaz. He was a good man who loved and trusted God. But the power of Assyria still loomed large, casting a shadow over the land of Judah. Hezekiah tried to keep his enemy at bay by sending tributes of gold and silver. He posted off the Temple candlesticks, and even emptied the palace of treasures. Then he stripped the gold from the Temple doors and doorposts. But it still wasn't enough.

After fourteen years of uneasy truce, the Emperor of Assyria laid siege to Jerusalem. He brought with him his very best generals. And once encamped around the capital, he sent a deputation to the main gate.

"Don't try to tell us you're relying on God", they shouted to the crowds lining the walls. "It's your God who has brought us here. He has told us to attack and destroy you. Anyway, all the nations we attack rely on their gods to defend them, and we've never been defeated yet."

There was a deathly silence all along the

battlements. Hezekiah had warned his people not to rise to the bait, and they patiently held their tongues. But the messenger who reported the speech to the king had tears in his eyes. Their situation was hopeless.

"Send for Isaiah", said King Hezekiah.

When Isaiah came, he brought good news with him. "Take courage, my Lord. The Assyrians won't fire so much as a single arrow at Jerusalem. The Living God will defend this city because His Temple is here, and to protect His reputation. As

for the Assyrians, they will be lucky to get home!"

Isaiah's words sounded over-optimistic, but somehow they had the ring of truth. The king and his people took heart. That night, the Lord sent a plague through the enemy camp. A hundred-and-eighty-five thousand men died in their beds, and the rest ran for their lives.

At first light, the sentries on the walls strained their eyes for signs of life. Nothing stirred. Gradually the truth began to dawn. The place was deserted. The Assyrian threat was no more.

Jeremiah

The danger from Assyria was over. But now a new empire began to emerge. Babylon! Her name was to go down in history as the conqueror of Judah.

God's prophet through the many troubled years of anxiety and exile was Jeremiah. He was very young when the Lord first spoke to him.

"Jeremiah, I have had My eye on you since before you were born. I have chosen you to speak My words to the world." And before Jeremiah could protest, God added:

"Don't say you're too young, because you're not! Just go where I send you, and say what I tell you . . ."

From that time on, Jeremiah saw things only too clearly. He saw Babylon, like a boiling cauldron, about to tip destruction on Judah. He saw that the Jews took God for granted. They thought He would never let them be captured because it would look bad for His reputation. Jehoiakim was king of Judah. He had his own plans for survival. Rather than rely on God, he tried to play off Egypt against Babylon. It was a foolish scheme, because Judah was bound to get crushed between the two.

*

Meanwhile, the Lord pleaded with His people through Jeremiah:

> "Remember the old days:
> The days when Israel and God were first married.
> Return to those days and be safe!
> Have done with idols –
> Lumps of wood and stone!
> Why wear your shoes out
> Chasing after them?"

The Potter

It wasn't easy being a prophet. Jeremiah felt God's anger like a pain deep in his stomach. Every time he passed a beggar, or saw a merchant giving short measure, he saw the certainty of God's judgement. Jerusalem was like rotten fruit, ready to fall from the branch. But the people couldn't see it. They ate and drank and pleased themselves. And as for Jeremiah, they voted him "Kill-joy of the Year". If serving God made you as miserable as that, you were better off without Him.

One day, the Lord spoke to Jeremiah. "Go down to the Potter's house, and watch him at his work. You'll see what I mean when you get there." So Jeremiah went to watch the Potter. The shelves were lined with finished crocks. But the floor was littered with smithereens.

The Potter was at his wheel, steadily working a lump of clay. Gradually it took shape. It became a beautiful vase under his hands. Suddenly, it developed a fault. The Potter broke it down and patiently started again . . .

"Yes," thought Jeremiah, "God is like this Potter. We are his workmanship. And when we develop faults, He has the right to break us down. We can hardly blame Him if He wants to start again.

After all, He is God!" Jeremiah stood there trembling. Was God looking at His people with a Potter's eye? Would everything that God had achieved – the Royal House, the Temple, the Worship – now have to be destroyed?

It wasn't easy being a prophet.

The Vase

Jeremiah bought the biggest and best vase in the shop, and headed for the Valley of Hinnom. Hinnom was the refuse tip where city folk brought their rubbish. On his way there, Jeremiah collected quite a crowd, including some city elders and a few priests. When he arrived in the valley, he delivered his speech.

206

"Rulers of Judah and people of Jerusalem, listen to the voice of God! I am going to bring destruction on this city. Everyone who sees it will be shocked and amazed. An enemy will surround it, capture it, and slaughter the population. Why? Because you have gone running after other gods. Because you have refused to keep My Law."

With all eyes on him, Jeremiah lifted the precious vase high in the air and threw it far down the cliff into the valley. It smashed into a thousand pieces.

"Listen to the Lord! I will break this people and this city. They will never be put together again. And when judgement falls on Judah, they will bury My people here – yes, even on the tip – because there will be nowhere else to put them!"

After that, Jeremiah marched to the Temple. He stood in the courtyard, and began to make the same speech all over again. But this time he had gone too far. The Temple police arrested him, beat him, and threw him in a cell for the night. Alone in the darkness, Jeremiah cried out to God:

"Lord, why did You make me do this?
Why do I have to preach?
Your message is like a fire within me.
How I wish I had never been born!"

The Letter

It wasn't long before Jeremiah's words came true. Nebuchadnezzar, ruler of Babylon, came and conquered Jerusalem. He did not destroy the city, but left a Governor there; and ordered the citizens to pay their taxes to him. In a way, life went on much as before, and the Temple worship was allowed to continue.

However, the king and his mother, the palace officials, and all the leading merchants and craftsmen, were taken into Exile. Nebuchadnezzar thought that by creaming off the leaders he would easily control the rest. And anyway, he wanted to keep an eye on them! Once in Babylon, the Jews began to despair. They didn't understand the language. They didn't believe in the gods. In the end, they liked nothing better than to meet down by the river and dream of home. And, of course, the dreaming led to tears. They wrote mournful letters to their friends in Jerusalem.

When Jeremiah heard of the state they were in, he decided to send them a letter in return. But it wasn't just another tear-jerker, with news of the Temple and other gossip. Jeremiah's letter was a word from the Lord:

"Dear friends,

Listen to the Living God:

"The damage is done. Jerusalem is captured, and you are in Exile. The best you can do now is settle down. Dry your tears, and get to work. Build houses and plant gardens. Marry and have children. It's time to stop living in the past, and show what God's people are made of.
Babylon's day won't last for ever. And I will certainly not forget you. I still have plans for your future. Plans to gather you up from every land, and bring you home again."

The Yoke

There was a phoney prophet in Jerusalem. His name was Hananiah. He was doing very good business with his prophecies, because he told people whatever they wanted to hear. Jeremiah came across him in the Temple one day, and stopped to listen.

"The Lord Almighty has spoken!" cried Hananiah, waving his hands in the air. ("So far so good," thought Jeremiah, "I wonder what's coming next?") "The Lord Almighty has spoken! The King of Babylon will soon be overthrown. Within two years our own king will return, and so will his mother, the palace officials, and all our leaders. They'll come in triumph, bringing with

210

them the Temple candlesticks and the royal
treasures. This is the word of the Lord."

There was a round of applause from the crowd of
listeners. "Great stuff, Hananiah!" they shouted.
"That's what we need to hear!"

Jeremiah slipped out of the Temple, ran to a
carpenter's shop and staggered back with a yoke
across his shoulders. Then, in front of all the priests
and people, he said to Hananiah: "Well now, that *is*
good news! The king and his mother back here in no
time, and everyone living happily ever after! You
know what we say about prophets who preach
'Peace'? 'We'll believe it when we see it!' " All the
time he was speaking, Jeremiah had the yoke on his
shoulders, the back-breaking symbol of Babylon's
power. Hananiah strode up to Jeremiah, took the

yoke from him, and snapped it in two. He was a strong man. "The Lord will break the yoke of Nebuchadnezzar!" he cried. "And he'll do it within two years. You mark my words!"

But Jeremiah said quietly. "Hananiah, you are mistaken. And if you encourage people to throw off a wooden yoke, they'll soon find themselves with an iron one! You are misleading folk with your so-called prophecies, and the Lord won't put up with it much longer."

Two years later the weight of Babylon still lay heavy on Jewish shoulders. And Hananiah? He was dead.

The Pit

In spite of all Jeremiah's advice, the people of Jerusalem rebelled against Babylon. They simply would not accept the Lord's punishment, but kept trying to set themselves free. Eventually Nebuchadnezzar ran out of patience, and sent an army to wipe them out. The citizens woke up one morning to find themselves surrounded.

Jeremiah spoke up. "King of Judah and people of Jerusalem! – You have no course but to surrender. If you try to hold out, you will all be killed – always assuming you don't starve first. So why not face facts, and give in!"

The Court officials told the king what Jeremiah was saying. "That man's a traitor!" they said. "He must be silenced at once. Look what he's doing to the morale of the soldiers. He turns their legs to jelly!"

King Zedekiah thought for a moment. "Very well," he said, "but don't kill him. Whatever you say, Jeremiah is the prophet of the Living God."

"Of course we won't kill him", they said, and rushed off to make the arrest. They took Jeremiah and threw him down a well. There was no water in it, just mud. And it stank like a sewer. Jeremiah sank up to his ankles. Then he sank up to his knees. Then he sank up to his waist. Then he stopped sinking. All the time, he continued to shout at the top of his voice: "Face facts, give in!"

If help hadn't arrived, Jeremiah would have died there and then. But a friend of his, Ebedmelech, got the king's permission to rescue him. With three others, he lowered some worn-out clothes for Jeremiah to wrap under his arms. Then they hauled him out with a rope. "Phew!" they said. "You may be a man of God, but you don't smell too good at the moment!"

"I know", said Jeremiah. "Can I have a wash?"

"No time for that, I'm afraid", said Ebedmelech, "the King wants to see you right away!"

The End

Jeremiah and the king sat face to face. Zedekiah smiled grimly, and lowered his voice.

"Jeremiah," he said, "we are surrounded. Our position is desperate. You are a man of God. Can you tell me what to do?"

Jeremiah sighed. "If I tell you the truth, you will have me beheaded!"

"Jeremiah," said the king, "you have my word . . ."

"All right, my Lord", said Jeremiah "Your best course is to surrender to Babylon. That way the city stays intact, and we all get out of it alive."

The king was trembling with indecision. "But if I give in, my people will call me a coward. There will always be someone who says we should have trusted God and held out."

Jeremiah felt sorry for Zedekiah. "Believe me, my Lord, this is no time to worry about what others think. God doesn't want you to be brave. He wants you to live!"

★

In the end, the king had his mind made up for him. The armies of Babylon attacked Jerusalem, and broke through the walls. Zedekiah made a run for it, but his enemies overtook him at Jericho. They blinded him and clapped him in chains. Back in the city, the houses and walls were torn down, and the palace was burned to the ground. Worst of all, the Temple was destroyed, and all the inhabitants were taken captive.

Jeremiah was among those caught. He was near to despair. "What difference did it make that I warned this would come? It still didn't stop it happening!"

Just then, a Babylonian official came over to him. "You're Jeremiah, aren't you? I have orders to set you free." With that, he took the chains from Jeremiah's wrists, and gave him a parcel of food. "You can come with the prisoners to Babylon, or you can stay here with the peasants. It's up to you."

Jeremiah was in a dream. He wandered into a nearby village. He could see old people sitting in the shade, and hear the children playing. It seemed that life would go on after all. He decided to stay.

Babylon

The sad procession arrived in Babylon. The journey had taken many weeks, and some of the sick and elderly had died on the way. In front marched the proud Babylonian soldiers. Behind them shuffled the captive Jews, gazing fearfully from side to side. They were still shocked and dazed from the sight of Jerusalem in flames. There was nothing for them now but a life of slavery.

There to welcome them were the Jews who had been taken prisoner years before. They were eagerly scanning the crowd for a face they knew. They anxiously asked after relatives. But apart from that there was silence.

The Babylonians on the other hand were in good spirits. "Come along now, cheer up you miserable lot!" said one of them. "This is Babylon, centre of the world. Consider yourselves lucky to be here!" "That's right", said another. "Say, why don't you give us a tune? You'll find us very musical in these parts – very musical indeed!" There was a great

218

laugh from the other soldiers, who launched into one of their drinking songs.

But the Jews were unable to sing. After all, their songs were about the City and the Temple. What use were such songs now?

"We sit by the river and weep,
We hang up our harps on the trees.
We sit by the water and long for our home,
We lift up our prayer on the breeze.
And how can we sing of Zion
To the men who brought her down?"

★

In the years of slavery, there was much heart-searching among the Jews. "It's all our fault", they said. "Isaiah warned us. So did Jeremiah. But we wouldn't listen. Our fathers went their own sweet way, and so did we. No doubt our children will be just the same, and there's nothing anyone can do about it."

But a new prophet began to plead with them. "Don't talk like that. God is always ready to start afresh. He can give us new hearts and new lives the moment we look to Him for help."

And that prophet's name was Ezekiel.

Ezekiel

Ezekiel is a tower of strength to the exiled Jews. He knew all about the siege of Jerusalem before it ever happened, and had felt the agony of it himself. Now he begins to speak God's message of hope.

"I see a valley full of bones", he says. "The bones are dry and broken. It's as if an entire army has been put to death and ground to powder . . . But wait! The Living God wants me to preach to those bones! Oh well, here goes: 'Listen bones! the Lord is with you! You're going to get your breath back. You're going to come to life!' "

All around him people are listening. Ezekiel may be nutty, but he's fun!

"No sooner do I preach to the bones than I hear a sort of rattle. Good gracious! The bones are coming together! Rib-cages appear from nowhere and skulls hop onto shoulders! And as I watch, the skeletons are clothed in flesh – yes, sinews and muscles and veins and blood! And finally – would you believe it – skin!"

The people burst out laughing. But Ezekiel holds up his hand for silence.

"I think to myself, 'So what? All I have now is a valley of corpses! What use is that to anyone?' And then the Lord says to me: 'Preach again, Ezekiel. Preach to the wind. Tell it to come from the ends of the earth and put breath into these bodies.' "

Ezekiel looks round his audience, and his eyes are bright. "So I preach to the wind! And no sooner do I preach than the breath starts to enter the bodies. They yawn and stretch and spring to life! And suddenly I have – an army!"

Ezekiel leaned closer to the people. "Do you hear what the Lord is saying? You may think the Jews are dead and gone, but you're wrong! Just you wait and see."

*

On another occasion Ezekiel said: "Listen! In the old days Israel was like a little girl. God looked after her, and she depended on Him in every way. She grew up to be very beautiful, and they were married. But then Israel turned sour. Sour. She thought she could do better elsewhere, and began to love other gods. Now she is old and broken, defeated and near to death. But hear what God says. 'Israel, I still love you. I love you as much as I ever did. Now won't you come back to me?'"

Jonah

There was once a man named Jonah. He was a Jew, and proud to be so. He wore Jewish clothes, he ate Jewish food, and he said Jewish prayers. Indeed, he had no time for anyone who wasn't a Jew: God loved the Jews, more than any other nation in the world. And Jews were best!

Jonah was a prophet, in a small way. At least, he claimed to be a prophet, and that what he said came from God. But some people thought he was a pompous, argumentative little man, who liked to be proved right. The truth is that he was both.

One day God spoke to Jonah, and the message was as clear as crystal. "Jonah," said God, "I want you to go to Nineveh. It's a great city belonging to the Assyrians. Go and tell them how wicked they are, and that I will soon destroy them."

"But God," said Jonah, feeling argumentative as usual, "Nineveh and the Assyrians mean nothing to me. I'm a Jew. I wear Jewish clothes, eat Jewish food, and say Jewish prayers. They won't believe a word of what I say, and they'll tease me about my hat!" But God said, "Jonah, go to Nineveh!" And that was His final word.

The next morning, Jonah got up very early. He had decided what to do. He would run away from God, and go where nobody knew him. He packed a bag, and slipped out of the house while it was still dark. By breakfast time, he was in Jaffa. It was a large port with ships to take you anywhere in the world. Jonah ordered a cup of hot milk, and thought carefully. Yes. He would go to Spain. Spain was about as far away from Nineveh as possible, and that was exactly where he wanted to be!

"Excuse me," said the waiter, "aren't you the prophet Jonah? Can I have your autograph for my niece?" "Er, no", said Jonah. "There must be some mistake. I'm not a prophet, goodness me, no. In fact I'm not religious at all!" He gave a short laugh. "Well, you've got the biggest Jewish hat I've ever seen", said the waiter. "Oh, the hat!" said Jonah,

snatching it off and stuffing it in his bag. "That was just a joke. I'd forgotten I was wearing it!"

An hour later, Jonah found a ship, bought a ticket to Spain, and walked carefully up the gang-plank.

He breathed a sigh of relief as the crew cast off. "Steady as she goes!" shouted the captain, touching wood and crossing himself. He seemed a very nervous little chap.

Being a landlubber, Jonah tended to get in the way. So he decided to make himself scarce, and leave the sailors to do their work. He crept into the fo'c'sle and lay there, enjoying the rolling motion of the ship. He also enjoyed the darkness. God would never find him here! He fell asleep.

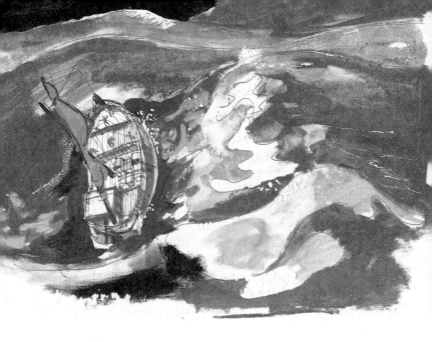

The Storm

The next thing Jonah knew, the nervous little captain was shaking him to wake up. The ship was pitching to and fro in a howling gale, and water was pouring through the portholes.

"Wake up, sir, for goodness sake!" cried the captain. "Get up on deck and pray to whichever god you believe in. Someone up there doesn't like us, not one bit." His teeth were chattering with fear. "We've done all we can – dropped the sails, thrown the cargo overboard, and turned to run with the wind. If that doesn't work, we're done for!"

Jonah staggered up on deck, and was immediately swept off his feet by the foaming water. The sailors helped him up. "We're taking it in turns

227

to throw dice", they shouted in his ear. "We want to find out who's in trouble with the gods. You're just in time for your turn."

Jonah shook the dice, shut his eyes, and threw. He knew what it was without looking. A one! The sailors gave cries of anger, and gathered round him.

"I think I'd better explain", said Jonah. "This storm is all my fault. You see, I'm a prophet on the run from God. I'm a Jew, and we only have one God. He told me to go somewhere, but I came here. Now He's angry." Jonah hung his head. "The best thing you can do is throw me overboard. That way you'll all be spared. In any case, I want to die."

"Well," said the captain, "I've sailed the sea man and boy for fifty years, and I never heard the likes of this." He touched wood and crossed himself. "But

if you're sure it's your fault, then we've no choice but to do as you say." He turned to the crew. "All right lads, heave ho and up he rises!"

Four strong sailors took Jonah by his arms and legs, swung him back and forth a couple of times and lobbed him overboard. Immediately the wind dropped, and the waves began to settle. Captain and crew alike fell to their knees, and promised to serve the Living God for ever more, without fail.

Meanwhile, Jonah sank down and down and down, until he thought he would never come up again. And then a great fish swam out of the gloom and swallowed him!

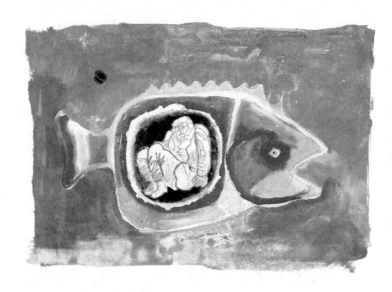

The Fish

"Help!" shouted Jonah, and very silly he sounded too. Whoever heard of calling for help from the belly of a fish? Jonah realized what he was doing, and chuckled. Suddenly, in the middle of the fish, in the depths of the sea, he felt closer to God than ever before. He prayed.

"Lord, I was running away from You, but You've caught up with me. I was tangled in weed and swallowing water, but You came to the rescue. Even in the ocean, You hear me as clearly as though I was in the Temple at Jerusalem. Lord, how wonderful You are! Whether I live or die, I will praise You."

Three days later, the fish ran aground, and spat Jonah out on a beach. He sat there, dazzled by the sunshine, and thrilled to be alive. Without waiting for another word from God, he set out for Nineveh. When he came to the outskirts of the city, he took his courage in both hands, and began to preach.

"People of Nineveh, the Living God is angry with you. In forty days He will destroy your city!"

To his utter amazement, everyone agreed with him. They came and shook his hand. Many of them had tears in their eyes (and not only the women!). "Thank you for coming to us", they said. "We've needed someone to say that for a long time."

The next day, Jonah walked further into the city. It was indeed a terrible place. The price of food was far too high for ordinary folk; and cripples, beggars and children were left to starve in the streets. Jonah preached again.

"People of Nineveh! The Living God can't let you get away with this. In thirty-nine days He will destroy you!" Again the same thing happened. Wealthy people stopped their carriages, got out, and started giving their jewellery to the poor. "That man's right", they said to each other. "We've known it for ages. We just needed someone to say it!"

Before long, the king himself heard of Jonah's message. He was cut to the heart. "If God destroys us, it'll be no more than we deserve", he said. He came down from his throne, threw his royal robes in a corner, and asked someone to find him a sack to wear. Then he sat down on the bare floor, and sprinkled his head with ashes. "I've sinned against God", he said. After a while, he went out onto the

231

balcony and spoke to the crowd.

"My people, we must join together in saying sorry to God. Let's all stop eating and drinking, and turn to prayer. Plead with God to spare us, in spite of all we've done to anger Him." Everyone did as the king suggested. They went home, dressed themselves in rough old sacks, and prayed as hard as they could. Even the animals stopped eating. They were all in it together.

Meanwhile, Jonah was beginning to enjoy himself. He liked being a thundering prophet, especially once people started to listen. How were they to know that at home he was just a quarrelsome little man with a big hat? He rubbed his hands in glee as he strode out of Nineveh. He wanted to make sure he had a good view when God destroyed the city. Only a few days to go now!

The Tree

High on the hillside, Jonah kept watch. Disaster Day came – and went. Nothing happened. No fire from heaven, no earthquake. Nothing. Jonah drummed his fingers impatiently. Then he scowled. He realized, of course, what God had done. He had seen that the people of Nineveh were sorry, and had kindly forgiven them. How typical of God. And how very embarrassing for His prophet! Jonah was furious.

"Didn't I always say this is what would happen?" he shouted at God. "Didn't I always know You were too loving and forgiving? You'd never destroy Nineveh, even if they are just a bunch of no-good Assyrians. I knew it! Why did you ever stop me going to Spain? I'll never live this down. I wish I'd stayed in the fish."

When Jonah had finished, there was silence. Jonah was surprised at how angry he felt, but he refused to take back a single word of what he had said. He sat sulking in the blazing sun, staring straight ahead, and daring God to give him heat-stroke. Quickly and quietly God made a shady plant grow up behind Jonah. It was cool underneath its leaves, and the prophet began to feel a little better. "I'm sorry I was rather hasty, Lord", he said. "Thank you for this lovely tree."

The next morning, disaster struck. A worm of some sort attacked the tree. In no time at all, it ate the leaves and the stem shrivelled. At the same time, the sun beat down fiercely, and a hot east wind seemed to roast him alive. Jonah's head was swimming. He felt desperately ill. "You've killed that innocent tree, Lord", he cried in defiance at the blazing sky. "Now why don't You take my life as well?" He rolled over and tried to hide his head. "Poor little tree," he said, over and over again, "you never did anyone any harm."

Then God spoke to Jonah. "Jonah, why are you so upset about one small plant? You didn't make it grow, and it only lasted a day. And yet you feel sorry for it!" Jonah opened his mouth to reply, but God went on.

"How do you think I feel about the people of Nineveh? I know they don't wear Jewish clothes and eat Jewish food and say Jewish prayers. But I made them, and I love them. Are you going to tell Me I shouldn't?"

The New Testament

Contents

Mary and Joseph

Mary lived in Nazareth, a small town nestling in the hills of Galilee. She was young, she was beautiful, and she was in love – in love with a young carpenter called Joseph. And he was in love with her.

One day, Mary slipped into the workshop to see Joseph. She was rosy cheeked with excitement.

"Joseph," she said, "I've got something to tell you."

"I'm listening," said Joseph, not listening at all. He was shaving a length of timber.

"Joseph," said Mary, "I've had a visit from the angel Gabriel – you know, God's messenger! He said I am very special to God and that God's Holy Spirit is very close to me and that I'm going to have a baby." Somehow Joseph had just cut himself. The plane was lying on the floor, and blood was oozing from his finger. But he was listening!

"It's not your baby, Joseph," said Mary, "I know we're not even getting married until next year. Joseph, this baby belongs to God. It's God's baby, and it'll be a boy. The angel even told me his name. We must call him Jesus."

While Joseph stood nursing his wound, Mary got some warm water and a bandage. She spoke softly.

"Joseph, God's doing something new. He's chosen us to look after his child. Jesus is God's son who will change the world. He'll stand up to the proud and wicked men who make our lives a misery. He'll help the poor and sick and weak." She carefully knotted the dressing. "Dear Joseph," she said, "isn't it exciting?"

Joseph looked at Mary. He was amazed at her courage and faith.

"Yes," he said, "it is exciting, though I don't know

240

what the neighbours are going to make of it all. But I had a dream last night, and I saw an angel. And the angel told me all about you having God's baby, and said I mustn't be afraid to marry you! So it looks as though we're in this together, doesn't it?"

"Together with God," said Mary, and gave him a kiss.

241

Jesus is Born

There was an Emperor called Augustus. He lived in Rome. He ruled the world. Emperor Augustus wrote a letter to all his governors: "I want to know how many subjects I have," he said, "and I want to know everyone's name and address – for tax purposes."

One of the kings who received the letter was Herod. He was anxious to keep on the right side of the Emperor, so he organized a census. Everyone in the country had to go to the town from which their family came. Joseph and Mary had to travel to Bethlehem, in the south, where King David had been born. They were related to King David.

Bethlehem was very crowded when Joseph and Mary arrived. All the rooms at the inn were booked, and they didn't have a tent. In the end, they took shelter with the animals for the night. And there, in the straw, Mary gave birth to a baby boy.

Even in the early hours of the morning, people came to see what had happened. Everyone agreed that this was no ordinary baby. There was an excitement in the air that night, the feeling that God was doing something special. The shepherds said as much when they came running in from the fields. "The sky is full of angels!" they said, "all praising God for this wonderful birth."

Mary remembered what an angel had said to her, not so very long ago. "You will become pregnant and give birth to a son, and you must call him Jesus. The Lord will make him a king, just as his forefather David was. But the Kingdom of Jesus will be better than David's. It will go on for ever."

242

John the Baptist

Jesus had a cousin. His name was John. John grew up to be a fiery preacher, like the prophets of old. He lived in the desert, by the River Jordan, and people spent their holidays going to listen to him.

"God wants to start again!" he would thunder, at the top of his voice. "You've taken Him for granted for too long. You've claimed to worship Him, but really you've been pleasing yourselves. Now it's time to turn to God and say you're sorry."

Many of those who heard John were cut to the heart. What he said was only too true. To show that they were sorry they waded into the water, and John gave them a wash. That was how he came to be called "John the Baptist".

People were excited by what John had to say. God was interested in them. God hadn't forgotten His special people. Perhaps God was about to give them a king, someone to lead them to freedom. There was even a whisper that John the Baptist should be king, but he put a stop to it right away. "Good heavens," he said, "I'm not God's king. Certainly not. I'm just the road-builder, making way for the real king to come."

One day, Jesus came to see John. He listened to John's preaching, and then joined the queue to be baptized. John was aware of him straight away. "What are you doing here?" he said in astonishment. "You're the one I'm talking about. You should be washing me!"

But Jesus said, "I want to be with my people in everything. If they are turning to God, then I want to join them in the water."

All eyes were on Jesus, as he went down into the river. And while he was being baptized, a remarkable thing happened. God's Spirit came and settled on him – just like a dove fluttering down. And a voice from heaven said, "You are My own dear Son. I am pleased with you."

247

In the Desert

After that, Jesus went off into the desert by himself. He needed to be alone. He needed to think, and pray. What would it mean being God's Son in a tiny corner of the Roman Empire? What would he have to do?

After about a month, when he was very tired, and very hungry, the Devil came to test him. "If you are God's Son," said the Devil, "why don't you treat us all to some magic? For example, you could turn stones to bread, and feed everyone! We've always wondered why God allows so many people to starve."

"There's more to life than bread", said Jesus. "Men and women are hungry for God's word. You can't give them that by magic."

They came to the summit of a mountain. The view was breathtaking. After a while the Devil said, "All this is mine, you know. I have the whole world in my power. But if you agree to worship me, I'll make you Emperor straight away."

"But I don't want to worship you", said Jesus simply. "I wouldn't worship you for a moment – not even for the whole world. The Bible says we must keep our worship for God, and for Him alone."

"Well," said the Devil, "if you're going to quote the Bible, why not throw yourself off the top of the Temple? Scripture says 'the angels will catch you so you won't get hurt'." He smiled. "It would get you off to a good start – Son of God!"

"Scripture also says, 'Do not put the Lord your God to the test'!" answered Jesus.

The Fishermen

Meet Simon. That's him with the fishing net. He lives in the town of Capernaum, on the shore of Galilee. Jesus has come to live there recently, and there's a lot of talk about him. But Simon hasn't had time to take much notice. He has to fish at night, which means that he's asleep during the day – asleep, or checking his tackle.

One day, in the misty light of dawn, Jesus stopped by. "How did you get on last night,

249

Simon?", he said. Simon looked up. He smiled
ruefully.

"To be honest, I didn't catch a thing", he
replied. "Absolutely nothing, unless you count a
few sardines and an old boot."

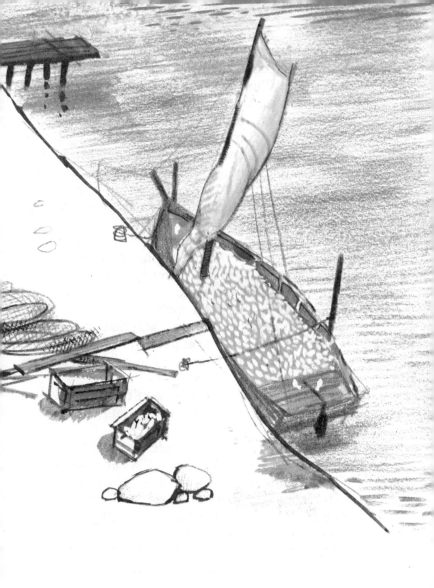

Jesus had to laugh. "Look here," he said, "I'll come with you. Try that deeper water over there,

251

and let down your nets just once more."

Simon shrugged. They said Jesus used to be a carpenter. What did he know about fishing? Oh well, anything for a quiet life . . . A few minutes later, they were out on Galilee. The sun was rising higher, and Simon was impatient. "This is ridiculous! Who ever heard of trying to fish in deep water in broad daylight?" But he cast the net all the same. He counted to ten, and started to pull it in. For some reason it seemed rather sluggish. Perhaps he was just tired.

And then he saw the net. It was absolutely teeming with silver fish, flapping and jumping in their attempts to get free. Peter had been fishing on Galilee for years, ever since he was a boy. He had never in all his life seen such a catch. Hastily, he signalled other boats to come and take the strain.

Then he fell to his knees in front of Jesus. "Lord, you must leave me. I'm not fit to mix with such as you."

But Jesus said, "Simon, don't be afraid. I've helped you with your work, will you help me with mine?"

Simon looked at Jesus, wide-eyed. "My work is catching fish", he said slowly. "What's yours?"

Jesus smiled. "My work is catching men", he said. "That's an all-weather job, too. And it needs patience." He looked at Simon. "Will you come?"

So Simon beached his boat for the last time, and went with Jesus. And so did his brother Andrew, and their friends James and John.

Flowers

So Jesus began to form his group of disciples. Apart from Peter and Andrew and James and John, there was Philip and Bartholemew – he also came from Galilee. Then there was Matthew, who used to be a tax collector, and Simon who used to be (and probably still was) a rebel! After them came Thomas, a twin, two Judases, and another James.

As they travelled from village to village and from town to town, they learned all they could from Jesus. They heard his stories many times, and watched the way he dealt with people. They all agreed, he was the most remarkable man they had ever met.

One day, they had stopped by a well for lunch, and were talking as usual.

"Well," said Simon, sitting back with a satisfied sigh, "when do we start?"

"When do we start what?" said Jesus.

"He means when do we start the revolution," said Judas Iscariot, polishing the blade of his dagger, "when do we proclaim you as King, and gather together an army?"

Jesus raised his hands for silence. "I keep trying to explain that I'm not that sort of king. I haven't come to put people to death. I've come to offer them life! You ask 'When do you begin?' My answer is, we *have* begun. This is it! Sharing our life, trusting God, and letting tomorrow take care of itself. Look at the flowers – do they worry about what to wear? And the birds – doesn't God look after them? So why are you fussing? Let's be glad that we belong to God, and leave our problems to Him."

Fruit

Jesus and his friends were hunting for figs. Fig trees have large leaves, and if you look under these you find the fruit. But the tree Jesus was searching had no figs at all – lovely leaves, but no fruit. Jesus pointed it out to his disciples.

"You know, this tree reminds me of some people I know. They look all right on the outside, but when you search for real goodness in their lives, there's nothing there."

*

It was a Saturday, the day of rest, and they were strolling to church. As they went, they picked ears of wheat, rubbing them in their hands, and eating the grain. The church attendants saw them, and bore down on them in a rage.

"How dare you work on the Sabbath Day. You know you're not to lift so much as a dried plum until after sunset!"

But Jesus said, "Now let's get this straight. The Sabbath Day is given to us to enjoy. You ruin it with all your little rules. It's a day when we can eat and sleep and worship and relax. And that's what we're doing."

*

In the village was a man with a withered hand. He
256

was unable to work, so he had to beg for his living. No one liked to touch him, in case they caught whatever he had. As soon as he saw the man, Jesus went over to see him. He took him gently by the hand and prayed with him. The disciples watched in amazement as the man stretched out his hand, and flexed his fingers. Already the flesh seemed to be filling out. They sat down and shared their food

258

with him. It was the first taste of friendship he had had for years.

Suddenly a church attendant appeared again.

"I was watching you just then!" he cried, shaking his fist angrily. "I saw it with my own eyes! You healed that man, and you did it on the Sabbath. How many times must I tell you that there are six days in the week to do that sort of thing, but today you just rest!"

Jesus spoke softly to his disciples. "If the Sabbath is God's day, then the best way of keeping it is to do His will. He wants people to be healed, so that's what I do. As for that man," he nodded in the direction of the attendant, "I'm afraid he's just a fig leaf!"

Two Houses

Jesus said to his friends, "I want to tell you something. You know, when I talk to people, they all hear what I say, but they don't all do it. Someone who hears my word and obeys me, is like a man building a house on rock. It may not be a very big house. It may not be a very good-looking house. But

when winter comes, and the rains fall and the floods rise and the winds blow, that house will stay standing."

He looked at Simon Peter, "Why will the house stay standing, Peter?" he asked. "Because it's built on a rock", said Peter. "That's right", said Jesus. "Keep learning at this rate and you'll be as steady as a rock yourself!"

Jesus went on. "Now some people hear my teaching, and take not a blind bit of notice. Someone who does that is like a man who built his house on sand. It may be a very large house. It may be a very good-looking house. But when winter comes, and the rains fall and the floods rise and the winds blow, that house will collapse."

He looked at Judas Iscariot. "Why will it collapse, Judas?" "Because it was only built on sand", said Judas. "That's right", said Jesus, and looked very thoughtful.

"What is it you want us to do?" asked James and John, who liked to be active. "I want you to love people", said Jesus. "Not just your friends. Anyone can do that. I want you to love your enemies. I want you to be generous. Don't only give to those who can pay you back. Don't only have folk for supper who will invite you in return. I want you to show God's love in action. Care for the poor, feed the hungry, clothe the naked, visit the prisoner, comfort the sad . . ."

"It sounds like a whole new way of life", said Andrew in amazement.

"It is", said Jesus. "It's the way of life in the Kingdom of God."

The Madman

Jesus and his friends had crossed the Sea of Galilee. They were just stepping ashore, when they caught sight of a wild man nearby. He was running in and out of some burial caves. Running and hiding. Running and hiding. They stood still, and he came nearer. They could see that his hair was long, his body was cut and bruised, and he was completely naked. He came stumbling towards Jesus, and threw himself at his feet.

"Jesus! I know who you are! Please don't hurt me."

Peter tried to explain. "Master, we have heard about this man. He's Mad Mob of Gadara. He needs to be put in prison, but no chains or ropes will hold him."

"He's already in prison", said Jesus. "He's a prisoner of the Devil." He looked at the madman, rolling on the ground and foaming at the mouth.

"What's your name?" he asked.

"Who cares about my name?" shouted the man. "I'm just a Mob, Mad Mob!"

"No you're not", said Jesus. "You're a human being, and God loves you. I'm setting you free." He spoke loudly and clearly. "All you evil spirits, get out of him and go where you belong!"

At that moment, a whole herd of pigs stampeded off down the slope and disappeared into the sea. Mob sat up. He parted the hair from his eyes and looked at Jesus. "My head is clear", he said. "What got into those pigs?"

"Your evil spirits", said Jesus. "Come on, let's get you a bath and find some clothes."

Jairus's Daughter

Back in Capernaum, Jesus was met by a large crowd. Dozens of people had been waiting to see him. Some wanted to ask him questions. Some wanted healing. Many simply came to look. In that crowd, struggling to get to Jesus, was a man by the name of Jairus. He was well-known in Capernaum

as the person who looked after the church. He had often invited Jesus to speak at the Sabbath service. But today he was a very different Jairus from the one who unlocked the door and gave out the hymn books. Today he was desperate. When he finally reached Jesus, he threw himself at the Master's feet.

"Jesus!" he gasped. "Please come to my house. My little girl is dying – and she's only twelve!"

"Of course," said Jesus, "I'll come straight away."

But that was easier said than done. Precious minutes were lost as he got delayed by one person after another. "Come on, come on!" pleaded Jairus, wringing his hands. "These people have had their life. My daughter's is still ahead of her."

Finally, a message came from Jairus's home. "Don't bother Jesus any more. Your little girl has just died. She passed away very peacefully."

Jesus laid a hand on Jairus's arm. "Don't be afraid, my friend", he said. "Trust God, and all will be well."

When they arrived at the house, they found any number of women in the living room, weeping and wailing. Jesus pushed them gently outside. "Now, now, calm down everyone. She's only asleep. Let's have a little peace and quiet, shall we?" Naturally the women were most offended. After all, they took a pride in their funeral lament. Many people said they were the best in the country.

Jesus took the father and mother upstairs, and went into the girl's bedroom. He sat on the bed and took her hand. Then he called her. "Little girl! It's time to get up!"

Hearing Jesus, her eyes opened. She smiled. She

started to clamber out of bed. "There now", said
Jesus. "I think some lunch is called for. We've all
had a very busy morning."

The Storm

One day Jesus and his friends were sailing across the sea of Galilee. It was a lovely afternoon when

they set out, and Jesus was glad of a break from the crowds. He lay down in the bottom of the boat and was soon fast asleep.

Suddenly, a storm sprang up. It was the sort of

storm for which Galilee is famous – short, sharp, and dangerous. Even the most experienced fishermen can be caught, capsized, and even drowned. In no time at all, the wind came rushing across the water, whipping up the waves. The little boat heeled over, the canvas far too heavy, and already beyond control. And then the storm began in earnest.

The disciples were terrified – not least the sailors among them. There was no way they were going to survive in weather like this. And then they noticed Jesus. He was sound asleep, as though nothing was happening.

Desperately they shook him. "Master! Wake up! We're all about to die!" Immediately Jesus was wide awake. He stood up, grabbed the mast, and looked at the chaos all around him. Then he spoke to the roaring wind and heaving water: "That's enough! Be quiet!"

Straight away, the storm died down. It ended far more suddenly than it had begun. But Jesus was more concerned for his friends than he was about the weather. "Where is your faith?" he said. "Sometimes I wonder if you believe in God at all."

★

Some days later, Jesus asked them a question. "You folk hear the gossip. What do people think of me? What do they think I'm trying to do?"

The disciples looked at each other and shrugged. "Well," said Andrew, "some people think you're John the Baptist, back from the dead." (John had been put to death by King Herod some months previously.) Philip added, "Others think you're a prophet. There is a rumour that you are Elijah, coming to prepare us for the arrival of the Messiah."

Jesus thought for a long time. Then he looked at them very seriously. "And who do you think I am?" he asked.

It was Peter who plucked up courage to speak. He said what they all thought. "Master, you are God's Messiah. The One who will save us." There was a murmur of agreement.

Jesus lowered his voice and spoke to them quite sternly. It was almost the voice he kept for evil spirits! "I am indeed God's Messiah," he said, "but you mustn't breathe a word of it to anyone. Is that understood?" They nodded. But they didn't really understand.

273

Mustard Seed

Peter was feeling very low. They had travelled many miles, listening to Jesus preaching, and watching him heal the sick. But still there were many more miles to travel, and many more sermons to preach, and many more sick to heal. At last he came out with what was worrying him.

"What's the point?" he said. "There's all this talk of God's Kingdom around, but where is it? That's what I want to know! We can tramp the roads until our dying day, but the work will hardly have begun, even then."

"I know how you feel," said Jesus, "I've often felt the same. We can't go everywhere, and we can't do everything. But look at it this way." He

produced a handful of mustard seed from his pocket. "Look at these seeds – the smallest seeds you've ever seen. And yet you can plant one of these, and in God's good time it becomes a tree. Yes! A great tree which provides a landmark for travellers, a shade for labourers, and a nesting place for the birds!" He laughed at the very wonder of it. "And all from a tiny seed. Peter, that's what we're doing. Planting seeds. Seeds of God's Kingdom. Don't worry – they'll win!"

★

One day, Jesus called the Twelve Disciples together. "Listen," he said, "the time will come when you must do this work on your own. So here

275

and now I give you power to preach and heal. I want you to go out to the villages in this area, and tell them God's Kingdom is coming. Be very simple. Don't take a lot of luggage – not even an extra shirt. Go where you're welcome, and eat what's put in front of you. And God be with you!"

Two weeks later, the disciples came back. They were glowing. "We preached the Good News, and healed the sick", they said. "And it worked!" "And people were so pleased to see us!" added Peter. "They seemed really keen."

"As keen as mustard?" said Jesus, with a smile.

Food for All

Jesus was now very famous. Wherever he went, the news travelled like wildfire and crowds gathered. On one occasion, at Bethsaida, about five thousand men came to see him, to say nothing of the women and children.

Jesus spoke to them several times during the day, telling them as much as he could about the Kingdom of God. He also healed those who came with sickness or disease. It was a marvellous and memorable time. No one who was there would ever forget it. But then they noticed the sun. It was already low in the west. In an hour it would be dark, and all these people would be hungry and far from home.

"I don't like it", said James. "Five thousand starving men could cause a lot of trouble. And we would get the blame."

"Then the answer is simple," said Jesus, "we must feed them. Tell them all to sit down." He turned to Andrew, "How much food do we have?"

"Just five loaves of bread and two small fishes", said Andrew. "They come from a lad who says you're welcome to them if they're any help."

"Thank you", said Jesus. He took the food in his hands, and said a short prayer. "Thank you, Father, for providing for all our needs." Then he broke up the bread and fish, and asked the disciples to pass it round.

Well, the outcome was that they all had enough to eat. More than enough: they had plenty! When the crowd had gone home and the disciples were clearing up, it took twelve baskets to contain the crumbs left over.

281

The Accident

Everyone was talking about the same thing. There had been a terrible accident in Siloam. A tower, which was nearly finished, had suddenly toppled and crashed to the ground. Eighteen men who were working on the building at the time had been killed, and many more injured. Rescue teams were searching the rubble as quickly as they could, while

friends and relatives waited for news. The whole
affair had stunned the nation. Jesus and his friends
were talking about it, when a fat man interrupted
them.

"Those fellows had it coming to them. They got
what they deserved. You just can't get the
workmanship these days. I dare say they forgot to
dig foundations, or made a mess of the brickwork.
It's God's judgement on them for being bone-idle."

Someone else joined in. "I think that's rather
hard. I bet they took very good care with the

283

foundations and the brickwork. The trouble is, accidents will happen. When you go, you go! That's all there is to it." He gave a shrug of the shoulders and looked for the others to agree.

But Jesus didn't agree with either of them. He spoke very thoughtfully. "I don't believe God caused that tower to fall, not for a moment. God wants people to live, not die. It's not His will women should be widowed and children left without a father. God is more sad about this disaster than any of us."

He went on. "And just think what you've been saying. All right, there may have been some ignorance or carelessness on the part of those workmen. We don't know. But were they somehow

284

worse than everyone else, that they should die?
Were they worse than unfair judges, or cheating
shop-keepers, or bullying soldiers? I hardly think
so! If you believe they got what they deserved,
you'd better look out for yourselves!"

Jesus looked at the fat man. "God made us all",
he said. "He made us and He loves us. He knows
when a little sparrow falls to the earth, never mind
an entire tower. But a man's life is more precious to
Him than a sparrow or a tower."

The Rich Young Man

They were having a quick meal before leaving
Jericho, when they heard the thunder of hooves.
They looked up to see a young man arriving. He
brought his horse to a standstill and dismounted, all
in one movement. Then he hurried over to their
table. They stared at his clothes. They stared at the
horse. They had never seen such finery! People
passing by paused to watch what would happen.

Without warning, the young man fell at Jesus's
feet. He was fighting to get his breath. He knew

286

Jesus was leaving town, and he'd been desperately anxious to catch him. "Good Master, I've come to ask a question", he said at last.

Jesus brought another chair to the table. "Come and sit down", he said. "What is it you'd like to know?"

"Good Master, I want to know this. What must I do to live?" He caught sight of some knowing smiles among the disciples. "Oh, of course, I know I must eat and breathe and do my work", he added. "But what can I do to get right with God?"

Jesus thought for a moment. "I wonder why you

keep calling me 'Good Master'?" he said. "Only God is good. And God has told us how we can be good. He has given us the Ten Commandments; don't kill or steal, don't lie, respect your elders . . ."

"Yes, yes," said the young man, "I've done all those things. But I'm still empty inside. I'm still not really living."

Jesus looked at him. He saw through all the wealth, the fine clothes and the jewels. He wasn't impressed by the horse, even though it was the best in town and had a gold harness. What he saw was one aimless young man, a young man trapped by comfort and money. A young man in need. Jesus smiled at him.

"You know, you've had good schooling and a good home. You can run your family business and live in luxury for the rest of your days, if you want to. But I believe there's one more thing you need to do."

"What is it?" asked the young man eagerly. "Whatever it is, I'll do it."

Jesus said solemnly, "Sell everything you have, give all the money to the poor, and take to the road with us. We don't always eat, we're not always warm and dry, but," he looked at his disciples, "but we really live!"

When the young man heard what Jesus had to say, his face fell. There was a long silence. "I can't do it", he said at last. "I know I'm not happy as I am. But I can't afford to change." He got up and went over to his horse. Without looking back, he took the bridle and walked slowly away.

At last Peter spoke. "We've left everything to follow you, haven't we, Lord?"

"Yes, you have", said Jesus. "But then you didn't have so much to lose. When you're very rich, it's almost impossible to let it all go, and trust God."

Zacchaeus

Zacchaeus glanced at the office clock. Yes, he had two more minutes. He must leave at four to see the procession. Meanwhile, he would just check the money again, and lock it up for the night.

Zacchaeus was the Chief Tax Collector in Jericho. It was he who made sure that the local people paid their taxes to the Emperor in Rome. This money was used to keep the Roman Army, and the Jews hated paying it. They also hated Zacchaeus for collecting it. He was a nasty, greedy little turncoat. He was a cheat, too, because he demanded much more than he should, and kept plenty for himself. But Zacchaeus didn't mind. After all, he was rich. And when you're rich, who needs friends? At least, that was what he kept telling himself. But, deep inside, he was very, very lonely.

He looked at the clock again, locked the safe, and hurried out. Jesus was due in Jericho that evening, and Zacchaeus wanted to catch a glimpse. Was it true what they said about him? That he was friendly with tax collectors? It seemed most unlikely. In the street, the crowd was much larger than Zacchaeus had expected. He stood on tiptoe and craned his neck, but it was no use. Thinking quickly, he ran ahead of everyone else, and clambered up a tree. It was a sycamore tree, with wide low branches. He would be able to see Jesus without being seen himself.

But that was where he was wrong. A few minutes later, just as Jesus was passing the tree, he stopped without any warning, reached up, parted the branches, and said, "Well, good afternoon my friend! You must be Zacchaeus."

Zacchaeus was so surprised that he simply sat there, his mouth opening and shutting. When he finally found some words, all that came out was, "And you must be Jesus!"

There was a murmur from those standing by. "Come on, Master, he's just a nasty, greedy little turncoat. He works for the Romans. Now please come this way. The Chief Rabbi is expecting you for supper and there are several important guests."

But Jesus wasn't in any hurry. "You go on without me," he said, "I'm dining with Zacchaeus this evening." He smiled up through the sycamore leaves. "That's right, isn't it Zacchaeus?" Zacchaeus almost fell out of the tree.

Later, when they were well into the third course, and had talked about many things, Zacchaeus said, "Jesus, I don't know why you should bother with me. I'm the most hated man in Jericho, living in the biggest, emptiest house. And you choose to come here. Why, there must be a thousand better people out there who would be delighted to have you stay."

"Maybe," said Jesus, "but I don't always go where I'm wanted. I go where I'm needed, which isn't quite the same thing. I long to find all those people who are far away from God. And when I find them, I want to tell them God loves them."

"Do you mean that God still loves me – a nasty, greedy little turncoat?" said Zacchaeus, the tears starting in his eyes.

"That's exactly what I mean", said Jesus.

"Then I'll start all over again", said Zacchaeus. "I'll give back all the money I've stolen – in fact I'll give it back four times over. And I'll sell half my goods and give the money to the poor!"

"That's what I like to hear!" said Jesus.

The Prodigal Son

The following day, Jesus met the Chief Rabbi of Jericho.

"I gather my company wasn't good enough for you yesterday evening", said the Rabbi haughtily. "I hear you preferred to eat with Zacchaeus. You know who he is, of course?"

"I know who he was", said Jesus. "He was a nasty, greedy little turncoat. A cheat. A thief. But not any more. He's now as true a son of God as any rabbi in the land."

"I don't know how you can talk such nonsense", said the Chief Rabbi.

"Well, let me tell you a story", said Jesus. "There was once a man who had two sons. The younger son came to him one day, and said, 'Father, when you die I will inherit half your money. So please can I have it now? I'd much rather enjoy it while I'm young.' The father agreed, with a heavy heart, and the young man left with the money.

"Of course, he had the time of his life. Or so he thought. He bought all the latest clothes, treated all his friends to drinks, and went out with one girl after another.

And then the money ran out. Reluctantly, he looked around for work, but that was hard to come by. There was a famine in those parts and unemployment was high. In the end, he took a job looking after pigs – the last job he would ever have dreamt of doing. But beggars can't be choosers.

Perched on the trough, watching the pigs tuck into their swill, he suddenly broke down. 'Even my father's servants do better than this', he cried. 'I'll go back home and ask him to take me in – as a slave.'

*

"But when he was still some distance from home, his father came running to meet him. He flung his arms round his son and gave him a mighty hug. 'My son!' he said, over and over again. 'My son, you've come home!'

"As quickly as he could, the father helped him to

294

the house and called for hot water and new clothes.
Then they had the party of a lifetime.

"But outside the house stood a silent figure. It
was the elder brother. He'd been working hard in
the fields, and had come home late. When he heard
that his young brother had come back, he refused to
set foot in the house . . ."

"Yes, yes, very moving story, I'm sure," said the
Chief Rabbi, "but I can't for the life of me see what
that's got to do with Zacchaeus."

"Maybe nothing at all", said Jesus. "Except that
you're behaving like an elder brother."

The Party Must Go On!

Meanwhile, back at Zacchaeus's house, more and more people were coming to join the fun. Zacchaeus

296

wasn't behaving at all like a tax collector. He was
sending out for more food and drink, and kept
pouring money into the laps of all those he'd
cheated. Quite a few beggars and tramps had heard

297

about the open door, and had nipped in for a good meal before Zacchaeus changed his mind.

When Jesus arrived back, he looked all round the house, and beamed. "You know," he said to his disciples, "this is my idea of heaven!" The disciples were amazed.

"You must be joking, Master", said Peter. "You'd never get this lot in heaven for a start. And the Chief Rabbi's missing." They all laughed at the very idea. But Jesus was serious.

"Listen", he said. "You know the story of the man who planned a banquet, sent out the invitations, and bought all the food?"

"That's right," said Andrew, "and then no one turned up. One after another they sent their excuses. Someone said he'd just bought a field and had to go and inspect it – as though he would have bought it without seeing it first!"

"Right!" said Jesus. "And another said he had to try out some oxen, and another pleaded he'd just got married." There was another laugh, and a good few nudges and winks.

"Well," said Jesus, "let me tell you the rest of that story. The man was furious. He summoned his servant and said, 'If my friends won't come to my supper, then we'll have to look elsewhere. Go out into the streets, and bring in everyone you can find – it doesn't matter if they're poor, or crippled, or blind, or lame. They're all welcome!'

"The servant did as he was told, but there was still food and drink to spare. So the master summoned his servant again. 'Go out of town. Go into the countryside. Search the footpaths and hedgerows and ditches. Go where the tramps doss down for the night. Go where the beggars hide. And when you find them, tell them to come to my party. You'll probably have to drag them!'

"And so the servant went. He told all and sundry of his master's feast. And at last the house was full. Full of needy people who answered an invitation."

Jesus looked round the room again. "And that's heaven!"

The Two Sisters

Jesus and his friends arrived in the village of
Bethany. They were invited to stay at the house of a
man called Lazarus. He had two sisters, Martha and
Mary.

Martha was a wonderful hostess. Almost too
wonderful, really – she almost wore them out with
her kindness.

"Come in, come in everyone", she said. "Wipe your feet, excuse my hair, never mind the mess. I'm sorry I can't shake hands but I'm up to my eyes in cooking."

They went in and sat down. Martha bustled round. "Now, what would you like to drink? Tea, coffee, milk, hot chocolate, or I've got something stronger if you'd like it. Hands up those who take sugar!" She disappeared into the kitchen.

With Martha out of the room, they began to notice Mary. She was sitting quietly, listening.

"Mary's my mother's name", said Jesus, trying to draw her into the conversation.

"I know", said Mary. And then she added, "You must believe in your work very strongly to leave your mother and family."

"I do," said Jesus, "and it hasn't been easy."

Just then the kitchen door burst open and Martha appeared with her hands full of dishes. "Here we are", she said, putting them down on the table, and passing round the plates. "Sorry to keep you waiting. Now who wants soup, and who wants stew and who wants both? Then I've got a little fish if anyone would prefer it. Does anyone not like cabbage?" Without waiting for a reply, she vanished again in a cloud of steam.

Jesus went on quietly talking to Mary. "You see, God must come first in my life. He must come even before my mother and brothers, much as I love them . . ."

This time Martha fairly exploded from the kitchen. She towered over Jesus, red-faced, hands on hips. "Jesus, will you please tell that sister of mine to stop sitting on the floor like a love-sick teenager and start helping me with the chores? Can't she see how busy I am?"

Jesus laid a hand gently on Martha's arm. "Martha, you're being wonderfully kind. The food looks lovely. You must have worked very hard. But look," he nodded at Mary, "your sister's a thoughtful girl, and she doesn't often get a chance to talk. She's much better off sitting thinking about God than getting all hot and bothered over the food."

Martha wiped her hands on her apron, and sat down with a thud. She brushed the hair from her eyes, and gave Jesus a reluctant smile. "You're right, Master," she said, "I should have known we'd be quite all right with biscuits and cheese. Then we could all have relaxed."

"Never mind", said Jesus. "Let's enjoy the food together now, and have a good talk. Then I'll give you a hand with the washing up."

Here Comes the Judge!

They were now getting near Jerusalem. The crowds that followed Jesus were very excited. They felt all this talk of the Kingdom of God would come to a head, once Jesus reached the capital. Many hoped he would be made King of the Jews. And many hoped he wouldn't!

Jesus told them a story. "There was once a nobleman who was going on a long journey. He was going to a country far away, to be made king. But before he left, he called his servants in, and gave them each £100. 'See what you can earn while I'm gone,' he said. And with that, he left.

"The first servant was delighted. 'Capital!' he said, which is exactly what it was. 'I'll buy two sheep. Let's see, they're £40 each. That leaves £20 for a sheep-pen. I'll buy the wood and build it myself.'

"The next servant was also very pleased. 'I'll invest in a donkey', he said. 'I know a man who has one for £75, and perhaps he'll sell me a second-hand cart for £25.'

"But the third servant was almost frightened of his new wealth. He was certainly frightened of the man who had lent it. 'I know my master', he said. 'He's a hard man. You can never tell what he's going to do next. If I lose this money, he'll probably throw me in prison for theft.' Then he had an idea. 'I know what I'll do. I'll fold it neatly and keep it in a box. That way I'll know it's safe, and be able to give it back when the time comes.'

"Time passed by. The first servant's sheep had two lambs. He looked after them well. Soon he had

a small flock, and was able to sell the wool and the meat. His £100 began to multiply.

"The second servant did a roaring trade with his donkey cart. He drove people home from parties, took loads of produce to market, and helped folk move house. The money came rolling in.

"Meanwhile, the third servant kept his £100 safely in the box. Every now and then he took it out to check that it was still neatly folded.

"And then, one day, the master returned. He was now a king. The very first thing he did was to summon his servants. 'Now then,' he said, 'what did you do with the money I lent you?'

"The first servant said, 'Your Majesty, I bought two sheep, and now I have a flock worth £1000.'

" 'Well done!' said the King, clapping him on the back. 'I can see you're a man with initiative. 'I'll put you in charge of a whole state.'

"The second servant said, 'Your Majesty, I bought a donkey and cart. I now have a business worth £500.'

" 'Excellent!' said the King, shaking him warmly by the hand. 'You're just the sort of person I need. I'll put you in charge of a whole district.'

"The third servant came forward, carrying his box carefully in both hands. He bowed, produced the key, unlocked the box, and lifted out the £100 note. He unfolded it, and presented it to his master with a flourish.

" 'Your Majesty, I know you're a hard man. I can never tell what you're going to do next. I was afraid that if I lost the money you would throw me in prison for theft. So I kept it safely in this box, and am now pleased to return it to you. I think you'll find it all in order.'

"But the King was very angry. And that's putting it mildly. 'But I gave you this money to invest! How dare you hide it away in a box? At least you could have put it in the bank, so that it could have been earning me interest.'

"He took the £100 note, and gave it to the servant with the sheep. 'Here,' he said, 'Keep up the good work.' Then he turned to the man with the box, 'As for you, get out of my sight!' "

As Jesus finished the story, he said to his disciples, "There's all this talk of making me king. But what are you doing with the Good News I've given you?"

The Neighbour

A man stopped Jesus in the street. They could tell by his clothes that he was a scholar. "I've been looking forward to meeting you, Jesus of Nazareth", he said. "Can you spare a moment to answer a question?"

"But of course", said Jesus. He was often asked difficult questions. Sometimes people genuinely wanted an answer, and sometimes they were simply trying to catch him out.

"Let me put it this way", said the scholar. "God's Law says we should love our neighbour; am I right?"

"Quite right", said Jesus.

"The trouble is," said the scholar, "that I can never quite decide who is my neighbour and who isn't. I love my family, and my friends, my fellow Jews . . . But I can't stand beggars and lepers and Romans . . ." He looked round for inspiration. "Well, that Samaritan, for instance, skulking along

309

the gutter. He's a half-breed who worships in a rival temple. I can't love him!"

Jesus didn't give a simple answer. Instead, he told a simple story.

"There was once a man, a Jew, who was on his way from Jerusalem to Jericho. It's the most dangerous road in the world, and he should never have been there alone. But he was. And it wasn't surprising that he got ambushed, beaten up, and robbed. His attackers left him for dead. Before long, a priest came by. He was hurrying to take a service at the Temple in Jerusalem. It was the greatest honour of his life, and he hadn't time to stop.

"The next traveller on the road was a Levite. He worked in the Temple, and liked to keep himself clean. It would never do to get dust on his clothes and blood on his hands. He took a cautious look at the man on the road, decided he was probably dead, and went his way.

"Finally, a Samaritan appeared on the scene. I once heard a scholar describe a Samaritan as a half-breed who worships in a rival temple. Be that as it may, the Samaritan got off his donkey and ran over to help the injured Jew. He stopped the bleeding, cleaned and bandaged the wounds, and gave the man a life-saving drink of water. Then he took him to the nearest boarding house, and nursed him through the night. In the morning, he instructed the landlord to look after the patient, paid the bill for the next three weeks, and promised to call back later."

Jesus paused for breath. There were some rather shocked faces in his audience. He turned to the scholar. "If you're having trouble choosing your neighbour, then ask yourself this question. Who can I help today? Who can I help at this moment? Never mind who they are, or where they come from, or what they believe. That person is your neighbour. God says, 'Love him.' "

The Stone

At last they came to the brow of the Mount of
Olives. There before them lay Jerusalem. The city
looked peaceful indeed in the evening light. The
rays of the setting sun caught the golden dome of
the Temple, making it shimmer and gleam. Jesus
looked. He had known this sight awaited him from
the moment he began the journey.

"Jerusalem," he said softly, half to the city, half
to himself, "your face is beautiful but your heart is
hard. You say you belong to God, but you always
kill His messengers." The disciples were surprised
to see tears rolling down his cheeks. They sat down
quietly beside him. Jesus began to talk.

312

"You know," he said, "the story goes that when they were building the Temple of Solomon, the workmen found there was one stone missing. It was the keystone that was needed to complete the corner. So they sent down a message to the masons in the quarry. 'Where's the stone for the head of the corner?' As you know, the masons did all the stone cutting underground, so that the Temple would be a place of peace. They kept a note of every stone they had cut. Immediately, they checked the record for the keystone. 'You've already got it', they said at last. 'We sent it up some months ago!'

"Well, the workmen rummaged around in the rubble. Eventually, after a long search, they found it. It was such an odd shape, they had tossed it to one side, thinking it was a reject. Now they tried it at the head of the corner, and found that it fitted exactly!"

Jesus said to his disciples, "I often think of that old stone. It wasn't what they expected, but it turned out to be the right one. And that's how it's going to be with me. They'll throw me out with the rubbish, but they'll have to reckon with me in the end."

*

Just then, two men arrived from Jerusalem. "We're looking for Jesus of Nazareth", they panted, out of breath after their climb.

"I am he", said Jesus.

"We've come to warn you", said the men.

"Jerusalem is full of pilgrims at the moment. They are here for the festival. The whole atmosphere is very tense. We're afraid that people will try to make you king, and that Governor Pilate will call out the soldiers. There could be a riot. There could be bloodshed."

"So what do you want me to do?" asked Jesus.

"We want you to go away", they replied earnestly.

"I'm afraid that will not be possible", said Jesus, "You see, I've been expecting to come here for a long time."

"But you might get killed!" said the men.

"Don't talk such nonsense!" said Peter. "No one's going to lay a finger on Jesus. We'll see to that." And the others agreed.

The Procession

"We want Jesus! We want Jesus!"

The whole population of Jerusalem turned out to watch him arrive. Not that there was much to see. Jesus had borrowed a humble donkey, and rode quietly into the city. He came in peace. Many were disappointed that he wasn't riding a mighty war horse, and calling for rebellion. They tried to give him the idea by spreading their coats on the road, and tearing branches from the trees. A cheer leader set up a chant.

"Who do we want?"

"JESUS!" yelled the crowd.

"Why do we want him?"

"HE'S KING!"

But Jesus rode steadily on. He made straight for the Temple . . . God's House. He gave the donkey a farewell pat, and walked up the steps. The crowd fell back silently, wondering what would happen next. Jesus entered the Court of the Gentiles, the place where pilgrims and visitors could pray, even if they weren't Jews. Immediately, he was accosted by a busy little priest.

"Step this way, please. Change your money here. You need special money for the Temple collection – no Roman coins allowed."

"Is that so?" said Jesus.

"Yes," added Judas, who knew about these things, "and they make quite a bit for themselves on the side."

Jesus looked round the Court of the Gentiles. Quite apart from all the money-changers at their desks, there were priests selling lambs, goats and doves for sacrifices. Their prices were outrageously high. And what with the shouts of the traders and the cries of the animals, there was little hope of people being able to pray.

Suddenly, Jesus acted. He overturned the stalls, and shooed the men out of their kiosks. Then he seized a whip, drove out the cattle, and set free the birds. The whole scene was chaos for about ten minutes. And then there was silence.

"This is God's House," he said, "the one place in the world where people should be welcome and safe. How dare you make it a hideout for thieves!"

The Last Supper

It was the eve of Passover. Jesus drew Peter and John to one side. "Go and buy bread and wine", he said. "We're going to have our Passover meal tonight."

"Here in the city?" said Peter. "Is that wise? You know the authorities are looking for you."

"I know", said Jesus. "But there is a man who will lend us a room. He'll meet you in the market and lead you to the place. It's up a flight of stairs."

Peter and John did as they were told. They found the Upper Room, and prepared the food.

That evening, Jesus and his disciples shared their last meal together. Jesus knew it was their last meal, and talked about many important things. He told them they must always put each other first. He prayed that they would stand firm in the testing times that lay ahead. And then he did something very simple. He broke up a loaf of bread, and passed it round.

"This is my body, broken for you", he said. Then, at the end of the meal, he took a cup of wine. "I want each of you to take a sip of this," he said, "and remember that my blood is shed for you all."

When they had done so, Jesus was very thoughtful. "I won't be with you for very much longer", he said. "I must go through all kinds of suffering in the next few hours, and be killed. But in the months and years to come, break bread and drink wine whenever you meet. And remember me." He went on:

"Tomorrow is Passover. Throughout the world, Jews will remember the way God brought them out of slavery in Egypt and made them a nation. Well, as from tonight, Passover will never be the same again. God is bringing you out of slavery. He is providing an escape for you from the prison of sin and death. But this time the sacrifice isn't a lamb. This time the sacrifice is – me."

321

"And me", said Peter. "We've come all this way together. I'm not leaving you now. Just let them try to stop me!"

Of course, that sparked them all off. Everyone swore he would die for Jesus. All except Judas Iscariot – he had slipped out.

Gethsemane

Late that night, they took a walk in the cool Garden of Gethsemane. It was a favourite place with Jesus, and they had often been there. Jesus seemed very nervous. It was as if there was a storm about to break inside him. He said to them, "Just keep watch here, will you? I'd like a little time to pray . . ."

By himself in an olive grove, Jesus pleaded with God. "Dear Father, do I have to go through with this? Isn't there any other way?" The sweat was streaming down his face. God seemed a long way away. "Father, all I want is to do your will."

Meanwhile, the disciples had fallen asleep. The travelling of the last few weeks, and the strain of the last few days, had left them exhausted. They woke to hear soldiers tramping through the trees. There were lighted torches all round them, and the chink of armour.

Peter leapt to his feet. "This is it!" he shouted. "Let's show them what we're made of!" He drew a sword. And then he noticed who was leading the enemy. "Judas!" he whispered. "What are you doing here?"

Judas brushed him aside. He strode over to Jesus, and kissed him on both cheeks. That was his signal, so the soldiers wouldn't arrest the wrong man in the dark.

Jesus spoke to him. "Judas, would you betray me with a kiss?" He turned to the soldiers. He could see there were several priests in the party as well. "Do I

have such a violent reputation that you have to
bring a small army?" he said. "And why come at
night? I've been teaching in the Temple every day
for three weeks. Why didn't you arrest me then?"

But there was no answer. They simply tied his
hands and began to lead him away.

The disciples were dazed. Every one of them desperately hoped he was dreaming. It was all so unbelievable. And Jesus was going so quietly. What about the Kingdom of God? What about their king? And then they panicked. Blindly, they scattered and ran off through the trees.

Calvary

At first light the following morning, Jesus was brought before the Jewish Council. The priests who had hated him for so long, now accused him.

"This man never says who he is. But he lets people think he's the Messiah. Really! Is it likely that God's King would be a peasant from Nazareth?"

The Chief Priest leaned forward and peered at Jesus. "Are you the Messiah?"

Jesus answered, "If I say I am, you won't believe me. But let's put it this way. What Scripture says about me is now coming true. You'll see."

The Chief Priest was getting angry and impatient. "So you are the Messiah?" he snapped.

"You said it, not me", replied Jesus.

"That does it", said the Chief Priest. "We don't need to hear any more. Send him to the Roman Governor to be executed."

★

The Governor's name was Pilate. He didn't understand why the priests were making so much fuss. They said Jesus was claiming to be King of the Jews. But then there was always someone trying to cause trouble. Pilate looked at Jesus, and shrugged. "Flog him and let him go", he said. "Tell him not to do it again."

But the priests insisted. "This man is dangerous. He has strong support in the north, and friends throughout the country. If you release him now, you're not doing your duty to Caesar."

Pilate was all for a quiet life. This whole business was threatening to spoil his weekend. So he gave in. After all, what did it matter? People were being put to death all the time.

And so Jesus was handed over to the soldiers. They gave him a beating, then dressed him in a royal robe. "Hail, Your Majesty!" they said, and pressed a mock crown onto his head. It was made from plaited thorns. Pilate wrote a label and sent it to be pinned on Jesus. It read, "This is the King of the Jews". For all he cared, Jesus could have been their king. Pilate had no time for the Jews anyway. The sooner he could get back to Rome the better.

Jesus was led out of the city through a large crowd. The same people who had welcomed him such a short time ago now jeered and hissed. "Some King!" they scoffed. "Let's see if God will help him now!"

On a little hill outside Jerusalem, they nailed Jesus to a wooden cross. It was a horrible death that was normally kept for criminals. While Jesus hung there

330

in great pain, the whole world grew dark. It was as
though the sun couldn't bear to watch what was
happening. The crowd was hushed. Jesus said a
psalm to himself.

> "My God, my God,
> why have you abandoned me?
> I have cried desperately for help.
> But still it does not come."

After three agonising hours, he took one last deep
breath. And then he died. But God hadn't
abandoned him, and help was on the way. As we
shall see.

The Road to Emmaus

Jesus died on a Friday. The following Sunday
evening, all the pilgrims were going home. The
festival was over. It was time to get back to work.
Two of Jesus's disciples were going to the village of
Emmaus. They were heavy-hearted, and heavy-
legged, and their talk went round in circles.

"Whoever would have thought it?" said Cleopas
to his friend. "Jesus of Nazareth, the man most
likely to save our nation, and he's snuffed out like a
candle."

332

"I know," said the other, shaking his head sadly, "I really thought we were seeing God do something new. Now I wonder if there's a God at all."

Just then they were joined by a stranger. "Hello," he said, "you two look very mournful. Had bad news?"

They both stopped in the road and stared at the newcomer. "Bad news? Of course we've had bad news. Everyone in the world has had bad news. Or have you been asleep since Thursday?"

"What do you mean?" asked the man.

Cleopas took him by the arm, and walked slowly along the road. "What I mean is this. Firstly, Jesus of Nazareth was the closest thing we've had to a prophet for four hundred years – apart from John the Baptist. Secondly, our rulers had him arrested. Thirdly, on the very day we expected him to be

made king, we had to stand helpless and watch him die. Fourthly, everyone's gone hysterical. Some women were running around at sunrise, saying the body had gone, and claiming they'd seen angels." He paused, impressed by his own speech.

"Well?" said the stranger.

"Well, it's so depressing!" said Cleopas.

"I don't think so", said the stranger. "Anyone who knows Scripture could tell you such things were bound to happen. The old prophets said as much in various ways, that God's victory comes through suffering."

They listened spellbound as he took them through the stories of Moses and David and Isaiah, and many others. As he talked, the Bible seemed to leap to life.

"Look," said Cleopas, "it's getting late. Why not stop the night with us at Emmaus?"

"Thank you" said the stranger, "I will."

During the evening meal, they talked again about Jesus. "You mean we were looking for the wrong sort of king?" asked Cleopas. "We were looking for a leader to overthrow the Romans. But all the time Jesus was doing so much more than that. He was overthrowing Satan and leading us back to God?"

"That's right", said the stranger. He took a loaf, broke it, and gave them each a piece. He poured a glass of wine and passed it round. Something about his manner made them gasp with surprise. And then they saw his wounded hands.

"Why," said Cleopas, "no wonder you know all this. You are . . ."

But the stranger had gone.

Without finishing their meal, the disciples left

the house, and ran all the way back to Jerusalem.
They burst into the room where Peter and the
others were hiding, and told them everything that
had happened.

The Empty Tomb

But the others had news of their own. That morning, three women had gone to attend to the body of Jesus. There had been no time on Friday to do anything but wind it in a sheet. Saturday had been the Sabbath, when all work was forbidden. So this was the first chance they had had.

When they arrived at the tomb, they found it was empty. At least, the winding sheet was there, but the body had gone. They were wondering what to

336

do next, when two men in shining clothes appeared.

"You won't find Jesus here", they said. "This is a place for the dead. But he's alive!"

"Of course!" said the women to one another. "That's what he was always trying to tell us. It was God's plan that he should suffer and die. Now God has raised him in triumph!"

Quickly, they ran to tell Peter. "Jesus is risen! Death couldn't hold him. The body has gone!"

The disciples were puzzled, and scared. The women-folk might have mistaken the tomb. The authorities might have seized the body. Peter went to see for himself. Sure enough, there was the place where they had left the body on Friday evening: a small cave with a stone ledge, and a boulder to cover the door. And there was the winding sheet, and the turban. They had collapsed, just as if the body had evaporated. He went back home feeling totally baffled.

"It all ties up!" blurted Cleopas, when they had all told their stories. "God has defended Jesus, and raised him from death."

"Rubbish!" said Thomas. "I'm sorry, but I can't believe any such thing. I saw Jesus die with my own eyes. No one could survive what he went through. And until I see him for myself, and hear his voice, and examine his wounds, I'll not listen to any of your scatterbrained theories."

At that moment, Jesus joined them. They shrank back, terrified, thinking he was a ghost. But he spoke to them. "Peace be with you!" He smiled. "Don't be alarmed. I said I'd be back, and here I am." He turned to Thomas. "It's me all right, Thomas. Would you like to have a closer look?"

They clustered round Jesus, hardly daring to believe their eyes. He was alive! They ate and drank together, and talked nineteen to the dozen. Once again, Jesus told them that what had happened was all in God's plan. He had been a perfect sacrifice for the sins of the world. He had freely given his life, so that everyone could be right with God again.

Finally, he walked out to Bethany with them, and said goodbye. "I'm going to my Father now," he said, "but I will send my own Spirit to be with you."

And then he disappeared.

The New Beginning

The disciples returned to Jerusalem, full of joy. Judas had killed himself after betraying Jesus, and the Eleven now chose a man called Matthias to join them. He had known Jesus well, and was a good person to make up their number. They lived together in a large house, with the women-folk looking after them. For some weeks, nothing much happened. Jesus had told them to wait for his Spirit to come. So wait they did.

Then another Feast came round. This time it was Pentecost, and again Jerusalem was crowded with visitors. Pentecost was seven weeks after Passover. As well as being Harvest Festival, it was the day the Jews thanked God for giving them the Law.

The disciples began the day by going to the Temple. They were squeezed in with all the pilgrims, waiting for the first service, when something strange and wonderful happened. It seemed that a gale began to blow. Well, it was like a gale. Strong. Invisible. It swept round the Temple courtyard, filling everyone with awe. And then fire seemed to lick down from the sky. At least, it was like fire. Warm. Burning. The flames fanned out, touching every one of the disciples.

Suddenly they were full of the Spirit of Jesus. They were no longer just his friends and acquaintances. They were caught up in his risen life. They began to praise God and, to their surprise, found that they were speaking all the languages of the world.

"Good heavens!" said someone who overheard them. "They sound as drunk as lords. And first thing in the morning too! They've been at the harvest parties . . ."

But someone else said, "No – listen! They're telling us about a great thing that God has done."

Peter jumped onto a low wall, and raised his hands for silence. He bellowed out in his big north-country voice. "I know you think we're drunk, but we're not." He grinned broadly. "And by the way, if you know a pub that's open this early, come and tell me afterwards." There was a great laugh from the crowd. He lifted his hands again. "Seriously," he said, "what you are seeing this morning is a prophecy come true. Joel told us that one day God's Spirit would be poured out on men and women everywhere. And this is it! It's all because of Jesus whom you saw put to death outside this very city less than two months ago. Yes, you killed him all right. But God raised him to life again. We knew he was special, because of all the wonderful things he did. But now we know who he really was. Who he really *is*. God's Son!"

When they heard what Peter had to say, people

pressed forward to speak to him. "If we've killed
God's Son, then there's no hope for us. What can
we do?"

342

"Say sorry to God, and believe Jesus is His Son," said Peter, "then come and be baptized."
And they did. Three thousand of them!

The Lame Man

Jerusalem was buzzing with the news. The followers of Jesus were increasing in number every day. They shared their belongings, gave away money, and worshipped in the Temple whenever they could. The Twelve were kept very busy

teaching the newcomers. Fortunately, the presence of the Holy Spirit meant that they were learning most of all from Jesus himself.

One afternoon Peter and John were on their way to the Temple. As usual, they went in by the Beautiful Gate. As usual, there was a lame man begging there. As usual, Peter threw him a coin.

They had done the same thing at one minute to three, every day for weeks. Suddenly Peter saw the man. Really noticed him for the first time. Really heard him for the first time.

"Help me! For God's sake help me!"

The two disciples stopped. They looked at the beggar. "What would Jesus do?" they thought to themselves. "Why, he would heal the man, of course."

Peter didn't hesitate. "Look at me", he said. "You've just had the last of my money, but I've got something else for you." He took a deep breath, and said it straight out: "In the name of Jesus Christ of Nazareth, get up and walk!"

346

Imagine the surprise of all three of them, to say nothing of passers-by, when the lame beggar did just that! In no time at all, he was standing, jumping, and walking around. Then Peter and John went on into the Temple, with their new friend bounding round them like a puppy. He attracted many a second glance. "Haven't I seen that fellow somewhere?" said someone. "I was just thinking that myself", said his companion. "I know his face, but I just can't place him. He's obviously as mad as a hatter!"

On Trial

The beggar caused such a commotion in the Temple Court that quite a crowd gathered to look. When it dawned on them that this was the lame man they passed every day at the Beautiful Gate, they began to praise Peter and John. Peter thought it was time to explain.

348

"My friends," he said, "don't look at us like that. We haven't done anything. If healing depended on us, this man would still be sitting outside. It was the power of the name of Jesus that made this lame man walk!"

"All right, that's enough of that Jesus stuff", said a burly policeman. "I have orders to arrest you."

"Orders? Who from?" asked Peter.

"From the High Priest himself", said the officer. "I'd come quietly if I were you." He beckoned the beggar. "You as well. Come along now."

They spent the night in a prison cell. Next morning they were brought before the High Priest's court. It was full of the same people who had condemned Jesus. The High Priest told them to come and stand in front of him.

"You are charged with healing this man", he said sternly. "What do you have to say for yourselves?"

"It's quite true!" blurted the lame man. "Look at my foot." He put it on the table. The High Priest winced.

"We didn't heal him," said Peter quickly, "it was the power of the name of Jesus. The Jesus you put to death!"

The High Priest twitched. "That's quite enough of that, thank you", he said hurriedly. "Clear the court!"

With the disciples outside, the priests put their heads together. "This is getting ridiculous", said one. "Dead men don't rise, and that's that."

"Maybe not," said another, "but whatever this new power is, it certainly works. You saw the man's feet." "And smelt them", said the first.

"We must handle this one carefully", said the High Priest. "We'll tell them to stop this Jesus nonsense, or there will be trouble."

They called the disciples back in. The High Priest gave his judgement. "We've decided to be merciful on this occasion", he said loftily. "We're letting you off without flogging or fine, on condition that you never mention the name of Jesus in public again."

Peter bowed. "Sir, thank you for dismissing the case. In actual fact we weren't aware that healing someone was a crime, but we're always willing to learn. As to keeping quiet about Jesus, that's one thing we'll never do. So no doubt we will meet again!"

When Peter and John were released, they had to tell the whole story to the others, from start to finish. The general joy overflowed in prayers of praise to God.

And the beggar? He was outside. Playing tag with the children.

352

Philip

One day, Philip felt prompted to take the Gaza Road. He didn't know why. There wasn't much traffic. Indeed, the place was pretty quiet. And then he saw a small procession coming. It was an Ethiopian Official, complete with retinue, starting his journey home.

Again, Philip felt the prompting. God's Spirit seemed to be saying, "That's your man. Go over and walk beside his chariot." Philip did so. He could see that the man was a very high-ranking Official indeed. As it turned out, he was in charge of

the Royal Treasury, and responsible only to his queen. Philip could also see that he was reading something: the book of the prophet Isaiah.

The Ethiopian caught sight of Philip. "Are you a Jew?" he asked.

"Yes, Your Excellency", said Philip.

"Do you know what Isaiah's prophecy is all about?" he asked with a sigh. "I realize it's important, but I can't make out what he's getting at."

"I'll gladly explain it, if I may", said Philip.

"Of course you may, I'd be honoured", said the Ethiopian, and invited Philip to join him in the chariot. Together they read about God's Servant suffering and being put to death.

"Like the sheep that is taken to be slaughtered
He did not say a word."

"Now to whom does this refer?" asked the Official. "It refers to Jesus of Nazareth", said Philip. "I'll tell you all about him. It's a long story . . ."

Some time later, when Philip came to the end, the Ethiopian spoke. "You know," he said, "I feel as though I've been waiting to hear this all my life. This is what I've been looking for. This is why I've been to Jerusalem and bought a copy of Isaiah. Now it all makes sense!"

The caravan was pulling up at a watering place. "Look," said the Ethiopian, "here's water. Can you baptize me in the name of Jesus here and now? Or do I have to wait?"

"There's no time like the present", said Philip, and together they waded into the pool.

354

The Young Saul

Saul sat at the front of the class. His eyes never left the teacher. He took in every word. Everyone agreed, he was a model pupil.

Throughout the empire, Jews took their schooling seriously. Wherever they settled, even if there was only a handful of them, they appointed a Rabbi. Under his guidance, the boys learned Hebrew, and recited the Law. Children were brought up very strictly. Their manners, their clothes, their food – everything about them was as Jewish as if they were living in Jerusalem itself.

And where was Saul? He was in Tarsus – a harbour town in Asia Minor. On this particular day, which was Sabbath Eve, the teacher was giving

out marks for tidiness and good behaviour. Saul came top, as usual, and was allowed to choose the Bible story with which they ended the week. Saul asked to hear about King Saul. The Rabbi laughed, and began:

"I'll tell you of the time when Saul was jealous of David. He was so jealous that he threw a spear at the young man, and David had to flee for his life. Well, Saul decided to track David down and kill him. He didn't want him coming back to challenge him with an army. In the course of the chase, the King came to a cave, and decided to stop for a rest. As it happened, that was the very cave in which David and his men were hiding. While Saul was asleep, David crept up and looked at him. Was God giving him a chance to kill the King?"

The Rabbi told the story in such a way that the boys were on the edges of their seats.

"Go on, David, kill him!" said one of them. "He tried to kill you!"

The Rabbi lifted his hand. "No, David didn't kill him. But he crawled very close, and carefully cut off a piece of Saul's cloak! Then, when the King woke up and left the cave, he suddenly heard a voice behind him. 'Saul, Saul! Why are you pursuing me?' Saul looked round, and burst into tears. 'David, I've been very wrong', he said. 'You would make a far better King than I do.' "

*

After school, Saul and his friends walked home together. Well, they didn't go straight home. They played hide and seek round a stone pillar for a while, and took it in turns to be Saul and David. When Saul eventually arrived home, his father had already come in from work. He was a dealer in tents and tarpaulins, and was also something on the town council. He had recently become a Roman citizen, which was a great honour. It gave him various freedoms and privileges, and involved the wearing of a ring. In due course Saul would have such a ring as well.

To his surprise, he found the Rabbi had called in to see his father. It was rather a shock, because they would know just how long he had taken to come home from school. Didn't it say in the Book of Proverbs: "Let thy roads be straight. Do not diverge to left or right"? Saul blushed. And on Sabbath Eve too!

But his father seemed not to mind. "My son," he said, "you will soon be twelve years old. That means you become Bar Mitzvah – Son of the Law. Our good friend the Rabbi says you will be too clever for him." Saul looked at his teacher, who shrugged his shoulders and smiled. His father went on. "So we've decided to send you to a new school. A school in Jerusalem, the school of the great Rabbi Gamaliel!"

Saul looked from his father to his teacher, and back to his father. He was so pleased and proud that he didn't know what to say. It was beyond his wildest dreams.

The Old School

Saul arrived in Jerusalem. It was all he had hoped for – and more. He was overawed by the beauty and splendour. The Temple, the walls, the palace, the castle. "Jerusalem is built as a city", he said to himself, as he walked around. The psalms he knew by heart seemed to sing out from the paving stones.

In the forecourt of the Temple, he saw learned Rabbis holding open-air classes. Anyone could go up and ask a question. Mind you, you might have to stand on your toes and shout to make yourself heard. Surrounded by the largest crowd was the Rabbi Gamaliel, the most highly respected teacher of his day. It was to this famous Rabbi's school that Saul was going. He could hardly wait for lessons to start the following morning.

Saul was put in the second form. That was the class for sons of wealthy parents who could afford to send their children to school in Jerusalem. Gamaliel didn't do all the teaching himself. Of course not. But when he did speak, he said the sort of things that made you fall silent. So simple. So deep. So true. Saul began to love the Law more and more. He listened round-eyed, open-mouthed, day after day.

★

Some of the older boys seemed to take God's Law rather too far. They used to show off their knowledge to the younger ones after school. "Little boy," said one of them to Saul, "I hope you are aware that when you are eating peas you should put every tenth pea to the side of your plate. It is written in Scripture: 'Set aside a tenth of all that your fields produce', Deuteronomy 14 v. 22. I trust you do this, little boy? Or didn't they teach you that in Tarsus?"

"I'm afraid they didn't," said Saul, "but I'll certainly remember it in future." The older one went on, "I suppose Tarsus was one of those places where they don't take the Law too seriously. The sort of place where people go to the synagogue just to look fashionable." His eyes narrowed. "We could show them a thing or two!" Suddenly, he smiled. "Test me! Ask me, what is a Nazarene?"

"What is a Nazarene?" said Saul, obediently.

"I'm glad you asked that", said the older boy. "A Nazarene is a follower of Jesus of Nazareth. Nazareth is a grubby northern town, and nothing good has come from it yet. Jesus tried to tell us that God loves everyone, even those who don't know or keep the Law. He went round befriending beggars, lepers, tax-collectors, Samaritans, and all the other kinds of riff-raff. On one occasion he said that, as far as he was concerned, the Temple could collapse tomorrow."

"Whatever happened to the rascal?" said Saul, amazed that anyone could treat the Law and the

Temple with such contempt.

"He's dead and gone", said the boy triumphantly. "Dead and gone. We saw to that!"

Stephen

After that, Saul seemed to hear about the Nazarenes just about every day. It was as though everyone in Jerusalem had to make up his mind, one way or the other. It appeared that there were thousands of people in the city who still followed Jesus. And a very lively lot they were!

One morning, Rabbi Gamaliel walked into the class very solemnly. He sat down, and the boys gathered round to listen.

"Mark my words," he said, "great deeds are afoot. We live in exciting times." He looked down at the eager faces. "I have just come from the Council

Meeting", he said. "We had all the ringleaders of the Nazarenes before us – every one of them. They say we killed Jesus, the Son of God. And that God raised him to life again, to show who he really was!" He paused. "Now, my children, what would you do? Have them put to death?"

There was silence. Gamaliel went on. "I stood up. I gave the Council my advice. Leave them alone, I said. We're always hearing the Messiah has appeared. Remember Theudas, who was killed a few years ago? And Judas the Galilean? They all came to nothing. But, I said, beware! Because one day the real Messiah *will* come, and we none of us want to miss him. My friends, I said, my word to you is this: leave the Nazarenes alone. If God isn't with them, they'll be a seven-day wonder and fizzle out. And if God *is* with them, far be it from us to stop them!" Gamaliel smiled proudly at his little audience. "And they agreed with every word I said!"

*

It was some months later that the Nazarenes were in the news again. This time a man called Stephen had been arrested. He was well-known for the way he helped the poor and the sick. But apparently he had been speaking against the Temple and against the Law. He was saying that people could now come to God through Jesus. The Law was incomplete, and the Temple was out of date.

Every day, after school, Saul and his friends went along to find out how the trial was going. "If Stephen wins," said one of them, "we'll have to pull down the Temple!" "And close the school", said another. One afternoon, as they ran along to the trial, they met a crowd coming the other way. They were shouting angrily, and frog-marching Stephen in front of them.

"What's going on?" said Saul.

"Deuteronomy 17 v. 5," muttered a friend, "that's what's going on. Take the person outside the town and stone him to death . . ."

Swept along by the mob, Saul and the others found themselves outside the city wall. Men were snatching up heavy stones from the side of the road, and making for a nearby pit. "This is no place for children", said one of them, rolling up his sleeves. "Here," he said to Saul, "you hold the coats!"

A few minutes later, the people had disappeared as quickly as they had come. Pale and silent now, they picked up their clothes, and set off for home. In the pit lay Stephen's body, completely hidden by boulders, the first Nazarene to die for his new faith.

One of the boys had seen it all happen. "He died asking God to forgive them", he said.

"Maybe he did, but I'm still glad he's dead", said Saul.

The Road to Damascus

"This is to certify that Saul of Tarsus has completed his schooling under Rabbi Gamaliel, passing with honours in all subjects. He is now authorized to investigate synagogues and arrest heretics, wherever they may be found."

Clutching his letter, which was signed by the High Priest himself, Saul set out for Damascus. He was now very learned, very confident. And he had a deeply burning hatred of the Nazarenes. The warnings and beatings in Jerusalem had merely served to scatter followers of Jesus. Now Saul had set himself the task of hunting them down and stamping them out. Indeed, he had sworn to murder them all.

It was noon as they came within sight of the town. The journey had taken many days, even though Saul had made everyone get up early and ride hard through the heat. It was as if he himself were on fire. Suddenly, he was stopped in his tracks. Something

like lightning seemed to pass straight through him —
a thunderbolt from a cloudless sky.

Saul was thrown from his horse, and fell flat in
the dust. He couldn't see a thing, just a darkness
before his eyes, as if he had been dazzled. But the
darkness didn't clear. And then he heard a voice.

"Saul, Saul! Why do you persecute me?"

His whole life flashed before him. King Saul
hounding David in the story at school. Gamaliel
saying, "Leave them alone". Holding the coats
while the mob stoned Stephen . . . He hid his face
from the glare. "Who are you, Lord?" he said. But
he knew the answer. A light was exploding in his
mind, which was already changing his life.

"I am Jesus," said the voice, "and you are
persecuting me Saul. When you hunt my followers,
and threaten them, and throw them into prison, you
are doing it all to me."

They helped Saul to his feet. He was a broken
man. The proud young Pharisee with the fiery eyes
was reduced to begging for help. They led him by
the hand into Damascus. Three days later, Saul was
still sitting stunned, and unable to eat or drink.
There was a knock on the door, and in walked a
visitor.

"Brother Saul?" he said warmly. "My name is
Ananias."

"Welcome, Ananias", said Saul. "God told me
you would come. You know, you were the first on
my list for arrest and torture."

"I know," said Ananias, "and I must admit I
thought twice before coming. Tell me, is it true that
you have met Jesus?"

"I have indeed," said Saul, "or rather he has met

me. From now on, he is my Lord, whatever that may mean."

Ananias came over and touched Saul's eyes. "Brother Saul, the Lord Jesus has sent me so that you may receive your sight, and be filled with the Holy Spirit." Immediately, Saul's darkness fell away, and he saw the friendly Christian face in front of him.

"Welcome to our number", said Ananias. "And now you must be baptized. I think we'll call you Paul."

New Life

Paul walked down Straight Street the following morning, with a song in his heart. The colours and sounds and smells flooded his senses. It was as if he had come alive for the very first time. He noticed the people around him – Arabs and Jews, Parthians and Romans. What a patchwork world! And God loved them all. He had sent Jesus for them all.

A few days later, he preached in the synagogue. Standing in his blue-fringed robe, he boldly delivered his new-found message. "My friends, Jesus is the Son of God! He is alive. I have met him." The Nazarenes lifted their hands in prayers of thanks. But not so the Pharisees. They were very annoyed. In a moment, one of them was on his feet. "We thought you had come from Jerusalem to

arrest the followers of Jesus. Now it turns out you're one of them!"

After Paul's sermon, things went from bad to worse. The Jews who had been his friends before now plotted to kill him. They couldn't put him to death inside the city, so they waited for the day he would try to leave. But the Nazarenes were a match for them. They hid Paul in a laundry basket and lowered him over the wall under cover of darkness.

Once back in Jerusalem, Paul tried to join the disciples. Not surprisingly, they were terribly afraid of him. His very name, Saul of Tarsus, sent shivers down the spine. And how were they to know if his story was true? It was far more likely to be a trick.

And then Paul found a friend. His name was Barnabas. He had met Paul in Damascus and heard him preach. Now he stood by him and explained to the Apostles. "Paul is our brother now", he said.

371

"The Lord Jesus has met with him and changed his life. What's more, he's the best speaker I've ever heard." (This last statement was a little far-fetched, as Paul was not really a very good speaker. For a start, he had a stutter. And something in his manner made people snigger. But it was nice of Barnabas to say it, all the same.)

After that, Paul was invited to many of the synagogues in Jerusalem. His favourite text was from Psalm 2:

> "I will announce", says the king, "what the
>   Lord has declared.
> He said to me: 'You are my son;
>   today I have become your father.
> Ask, and I will give you all the nations;
>   the whole earth will be yours.' "

Paul would look round the congregation. "My fellow Jews," he would say, "and you folk at the back who aren't Jews, but have come to listen. You're looking at me as though you don't understand a word of what I just read. But it's really very simple. God says that one day there will be a king who will please Him so much, that He will call him His Son, and give him the world."

They were still looking blank, so Paul explained further. "You know that God called Israel to be His chosen people, ages ago?" They nodded. "He gave them their freedom, the Law, and a land of their own?" They nodded again. "And then they wanted a king, and God gave them Saul, who turned out to be a disaster?" Yes, they knew all that.

"Well," said Paul, "after Saul came David. David was much more the kind of king God had in mind. And ever since then, the Jews have longed for another king like David: a man who would do God's will, feed the hungry, protect the weak, and give justice to all." They were with him now, hanging on every word. Paul continued.

"When Jesus of Nazareth appeared, he did those very things. He didn't wear a crown or live in a palace, but he did everything God's king would do."

One of the Greeks at the back raised his hand. He wanted to ask a question. "Mr Preacher, are you saying that Jesus was as good as an anointed king? What we Greeks would call a 'Christ'?"

"Exactly", said Paul. "I couldn't have put it better myself."

373

Food for Thought

It was a special day for Titus. He lived in the busy city of Antioch, where he and his Greek friends had recently become Christians. It was a special day, because not only did he have Paul and Barnabas coming to lunch, but the great Apostle Peter was going to join them as well. He was on a visit from Jerusalem to see how the little church in Antioch was getting on.

Titus had chosen a very nice piece of pork, and asked his wife to cook it to their favourite Greek recipe. It was a fine meal. And exciting, in its own way, because Jews and Greeks usually avoided each other like the plague. Jews were brought up with so many rules about what not to eat and where not to eat it, that they refused to dine with Greeks at all.

Peter enjoyed himself hugely. He was a fund of information about Jesus, the things he had said and the things he had done. Titus and the others lapped it up. When Peter told them how he came to the tomb on the first Easter morning and found it empty, they listened spellbound. At last they all sat back. There were sighs of contentment. Peter spoke.

"You know, I have to keep pinching myself to make sure I'm not in a dream", he said. "Whoever would have thought that old Peter Bar-Jonah would sit down at table with Greeks in Antioch, and tuck in to a joint of forbidden pork?" They all laughed with delight. "I know", added Paul. "The way Jesus breaks down all the old barriers never ceases to amaze me."

Just then there was a knock on the door. Titus's wife came in. "Visitors from Jerusalem", she said. "They heard Peter was here."

Peter leapt to his feet and tried to hide the remains of the pork under the table. But it was too

375

late. There, in the doorway, stood some very surprised messengers from James. They looked at Peter. They looked at Barnabas. They looked at Paul. They looked at the pork. Then they looked at Peter again. He was blushing to the roots of his hair.

"Oh, er, come in, I mean stay out", he spluttered. "We can explain everything, I can assure you!" He gave a pleading look at Paul and Barnabas.

Barnabas had gone to the other end of the room, and was pretending to be incredibly interested in one of Titus's pictures. But Paul's head was very clear. "Peter, you're being two-faced!" he said sternly. "I daresay you are an Apostle and a leader of the church in Jerusalem, but at this moment I'm ashamed of you. Two minutes ago, you were saying how good it was to share a meal with Gentile Christians. Now you've been caught by Jewish Christians and you wish you could fall through the floor."

While Paul glared at Peter, and Peter hung his head, Barnabas came to the rescue. He spoke to the visitors. "Try to understand", he said. "In a town like Antioch there are people from many different cultures and backgrounds. When any of them turn to Christ, we can't expect them to become Jews. Jewish laws, Jewish festivals, Jewish history – it doesn't mean a thing to them! They already enjoy the new freedom of Jesus."

"That's right", said Paul. "Of course, we still treasure the Scriptures. Moses and the prophets looked forward to Jesus coming, and they had important things to teach us. After all, Jesus couldn't do without the Bible, and we can't either."

But the Jews were still looking puzzled and

angry. Barnabas tried again. "Don't you see?" he said. "The Good News of Jesus must travel out of Jewish circles. Jesus said we must go everywhere and tell everyone. We need men like Paul to talk to Greeks and Romans. And if he's going to reach them, he must go into their houses, and eat their food, and speak their language."

Peter spoke. "Paul, you're right of course. And Titus, I owe you an apology. Please forgive my bad manners." He raised his head and smiled ruefully. "There's always something to learn in this new faith, isn't there?"

The next day, Paul and Barnabas set sail for Cyprus. Peter and Titus waved them off from the jetty. "You preach to Gentiles, and I'll preach to Jews!" shouted Peter. "And may Jesus make us one!" said Paul.

The Magician

Paul and Barnabas arrived in Cyprus, and travelled on to the town of Paphos. To their surprise, they were invited to meet the Roman Governor of the island, Sergius Paulus. He was a famous and intelligent man, always open to new learning, and very inquisitive!

As soon as they arrived in the Governor's Hall and began telling him about Jesus, Paul became

aware of a sinister figure in the audience. Indeed, it was a man he recognized – a Jew by the name of Bar-Jesus who had been expelled from Jerusalem for practising magic. Seeing Paul's startled gaze, the Governor took them over to meet him.

"Paul and Barnabas, this is my good friend Elymas the Skilful. Elymas is quite a character. He can turn water to wine and stones to bread. He's not called 'Son of Jesus' for nothing!"

"Our Jesus didn't have any sons," said Paul

stiffly, "and neither did he turn stones to bread.
That idea came from the Devil."

"Is that so?" said the Governor. "You must tell
me more about this Jesus. Do you mean to say he
didn't approve of magic?"

Just as Paul drew breath to reply, he was
interrupted by Elymas. "Don't listen to them,
Governor", he hissed. His eyes glowed red. He spat
his words like venom. "Don't listen to them. They
follow a fool-hardy peasant who was executed many
years ago. They are utterly deluded."

Paul turned and fixed Elymas with his gaze.
"Elymas, you son of the Devil! Your spells and
potions spin a web of evil over all who have the
misfortune to know you."

Elymas began to tremble. He knew what was coming. Paul went on. "I'm no magician, but I tell you this. From now on, you will be struck blind, and God will allow you to remain blind until you mend your ways."

Elymas hid his face in his cloak, turned, and tried to scuttle for the door. But even as he ran, a mist came over his eyes, and then complete darkness. He tripped and fell headlong across the floor.

Sergius Paulus was astounded. He had found the magic of Elymas strange but intriguing. But it seemed that this Jesus was a name of far greater power. And power for good at that. He asked Paul and Barnabas to stay as long as they could, and eagerly listened to all they had to tell him.

Athens

Paul was alone – and tired. Yet as he wandered the streets of Athens, looking at the huge variety of statues, idols and altars, his strength began to return. Not because he was pleased at what he saw, but because he was exceedingly angry. Athens was supposed to be the intellectual centre of the world, and yet these great minds toyed with a mass of unlikely gods. He strode from one to another: Hermes, Apollo, Dionysus, Artemis . . . The tallest of them all was Athena herself. She stood outside the Parthenon, thirty feet high, a mass of gold and ivory.

Paul talked to his fellow Jews about it when he met them in the synagogue. But they seemed to

have got used to the situation. "This is ridiculous", said Paul to himself, "They seem to believe in every god except the real one!"

And then, one day, some teachers who had been talking with Paul asked him to address the City Council. "They'll like you", they said. "They haven't heard about this Anastasis before. She's a new goddess, presumably?"

"She's not a goddess," said Paul in exasperation, "Anastasis means resurrection. Jesus Christ rose from the dead!"

"Oh, really?" they said. "So we weren't too far out, were we?"

On the Hill of Ares, Paul preached to the Rulers of Athens. "Gentlemen," he said, "I'm most impressed by your magnificent array of idols and altars. You must be the most religious people on the face of the earth. But there was only one altar that meant anything to me personally. And that bore the inscription, 'To an Unknown God'." He raised his

voice boldly. "I tell you, the god you worship without even knowing him is the true and living God. He made the universe and everything in it. He doesn't need you or me to build him temples or cook him food. Far from it. On the contrary, it is we who need Him!" He smiled, and quoted some Greek, "As your own poets have said, 'We are his children'."

He went on. "Now let me tell you this. The Unknown God has fixed the day when He will judge the whole world. He will judge it through a man He has already chosen, a man He has already raised from death!"

At that, the whole Council broke out in a ripple of laughter. "We thought for a moment you were a proper philosopher", they said. "You certainly had us guessing when you quoted the poetry." By now some of them had helpless fits of the giggles. They were trying to be polite, but it was really too much for them.

"We must hear more of this – er – some other time", said the President, and left hurriedly. "Yes," said someone else, "this hypothesis that someone who was dead was in fact not dead – can it be verified?" And then he couldn't keep a straight face any longer, and gave way to a deep gurgling chuckle.

Paul sat on the hillside, his head in his hands. How could he persuade proud philosophers to consider the truth of Jesus? And then, as dusk was falling, a few people came back to talk to him. One of them, Dionysius, was a member of the Council. And Paul realized that all was not lost. After all, the majority isn't always right.

Corinth

Corinth was the place where East and West met. It was a brash new commercial centre, larger than any city Paul had ever seen. Its people came from every corner of the Empire. Many of them were slaves, spending their waking hours loading and unloading boats, or dragging ships on rollers from one sea to the other.

Without friends or support, Paul earned his living by tent-making. In so doing, he made friends with a couple called Aquila and Priscilla. They were new to Corinth as well, having been told to leave Rome because of their Christian faith. And they were tent-makers! Together, they set to work in an open-fronted shop near the quay side. And as they shared their Good News with customers and neighbours, a little church began to grow. Every Saturday they went to the synagogue. There Paul told the Jews about Jesus. Some Greeks believed, including Stephanas and Gaius. But most Jews didn't like it at all, and soon banned Paul from speaking. The work was painfully slow.

As for the believers, they were a mixed bunch – as mixed as Corinth itself. There were dockers and merchants, sailors and slaves. It was hard for the rich to share with the poor, and hard for the poor to love the rich.

One evening, Paul was a little late arriving for the meeting. They had arranged a meal at the house of Gaius, and everyone was bringing something to eat. When Paul walked in, he could hardly believe his eyes. At the head of the table sat a few of the richer merchants and shipowners, enjoying a hearty supper, and drinking toasts to each other's health. At the opposite end of the room sat the sailors and their girlfriends, together with those who were unemployed, and a few beggars. Some had their packets of sandwiches with them. Most had nothing at all.

"Whatever's going on?" cried Paul.

"Ah Paul, there you are!" said one of the merchants. "We've saved you a place up here.

Come and try this claret, it's really very good."

But Paul was angry. "If you want to get drunk, then stay at home!" he said sternly. "This is no place for your little private parties. How can you sit there with plates full of food when your Christian brothers and sisters have only a few sandwiches between them? This is a Jesus Meal, a love-feast. We should be sharing our food with each other."

And so they gradually got the idea. Their love for Jesus made them into a family of faith. Rich or poor, old or young, men or women, they belonged together. Because they belonged to Jesus.

First Love

It was hard to be a Christian in Corinth. It was such an immoral place. The young men thought nothing of picking up a different girl every evening, buying her a few drinks, and spending the night with her. And some of them thought that was what love was all about.

One day, Paul had a word with some of the young couples. "When we become Christians," he said, "God starts to change the way we live."

"How do you mean?" they asked.

"Well," said Paul, "He shows us how to put each other first. If you only go out with a boy because he spends money on you, you're merely being his slave. He's buying you for the night."

"That's rather a strong way of putting it", said one of the sailors.

"But it's true!" said a girl. "Go on, Paul, we're listening."

"What I'm saying," said Paul, "is that real love seeks to give rather than to get. That's the sort of love Jesus showed, and it's the sort of love we should have."

★

Two of the young people at church wanted to get married. Their names were Fortunatus and Nympha. The boy's mother came to see Paul.

"Paul," she said, "these two want to get married, and I want you to stop them! They've only known each other a few weeks, they haven't a penny to their name, and they're far too young!"

"But they love each other", said Paul. "Look Livia, I know it's going to seem quiet when Fortunatus leaves home, but he has his own life to lead. If you really love him, you must learn to let go. The time has come for him to leave you and take a wife. No doubt they have a lot to learn, but they'll be learning together. Much better they marry and make a home, than spend their evenings kissing in the back alleys."

Livia was very shocked at Paul's words. "I'm amazed to hear you say such things", she sobbed. "And you an Apostle too!" And with that she swept out of the room.

Paul turned to Fortunatus and Nympha. "Listen," he said, "the key to a happy marriage is Jesus. Nympha, you must love your husband and look up to him, just as you love and obey the Lord. But Fortunatus, you must pay attention to Jesus

392

too. You must care for Nympha in the same way that Jesus cares for you. That means laying down your life for her."

The couple looked at each other. Being married was going to be very different from just going out together. Before they talked to Paul they thought they knew all there was to know. Now it seemed that marriage would be the adventure of a lifetime.

Ephesus

At length the time came to move on. Paul left Corinth, with Aquila and Priscilla, and set sail for Ephesus. Ephesus was the capital of the Province of Asia, a city with many thriving businesses, but also teeming with pagan priests and magicians of all sorts. The Temple in Ephesus was one of the Seven Wonders of the World. There pilgrims flocked to worship Diana of the Ephesians, or Artemis, as the

Greeks called her. She was a Mother Goddess carved out of a black meteorite, and covered with scores of breasts!

Wherever you went in Ephesus, there was no getting away from Diana. The people believed she had protected them for centuries, and brought them luck. There were any number of shops for visitors to buy souvenirs: Diana pennants, Diana plaques, Diana boxes. And, of course, plaster models of the goddess so that you could worship her

at home. Most attractive of all were the miniature temples, cast in solid silver – a must for every tourist!

However, Paul had not come to Ephesus to worship Diana. He had come to preach the Gospel. Once again he earned his living by making tents. But during the lunch hour, while folk were enjoying a siesta, Paul would borrow a hall and give lectures. For three years he taught in this way, and people visiting Ephesus took the Good News of Jesus back home.

At this time God did some wonderful things through Paul. Perhaps because Ephesus was a centre of magic, He showed the special power of the name of Jesus. Handkerchiefs and aprons that Paul had used were taken to sick people, and they recovered. Evil spirits met their match as well, and were driven out. But when some travelling Jews tried to do the same, they had a nasty surprise. A demon-possessed man shouted, "I know Jesus and Paul, but who are you?" And with that he jumped up, gave them a beating, and threw them out of his house!

Riot!

There was one man in Ephesus who had no love for Paul. His name was Demetrius, and he was a leading silversmith. His craftsmen supplied the miniature temples to shops all over the city. But ever since Paul arrived, trade had been falling off drastically. What's more, some of his work-force no longer believed in Diana, and had left to join the Christians. One day, Demetrius called a meeting of the workers.

"Brothers!" he said. "We're losing business. This man Paul is turning people away in their thousands. They don't believe in hand-made gods any more. But listen to me. If we go under, what will happen to Diana? And if Diana goes, what will become of Ephesus?"

Demetrius soon whipped his men into a frenzy. They formed a procession and marched out of the hall, chanting "Long live Diana! Long live Diana!" People left their shops and offices, and joined the mob in the streets. Before long the whole city was in uproar. "Long live Diana! Long live Diana!"

The crowd seized two friends of Paul's, and swept them off for trial in the local theatre. Nineteen thousand people packed the tiers and terraces, and the noise of the chant was deafening. Paul saw an opportunity. He tried to get to the theatre himself, to explain what Christians believed. But his friends held him back. For two long, hot hours they listened to the hands clapping and the feet stomping. And all the time the chant

399

went on: "Long live Diana! Long live Diana!"

A Jew by the name of Alexander tried to make a speech. He started to say that the Jews didn't believe Paul's message either, but he was shouted down. This was a meeting of Ephesians in defence of their goddess. They didn't want to hear from any foreigners, least of all a Jew.

At last the Town Clerk was able to calm the crowd. He talked quietly, so that they had to stop chanting in order to hear him. "Honoured citizens of Ephesus," he said, "there's no need for all this fuss. Everyone knows that our city is the one true centre of the goddess Diana. No one can take the sacred statue from us, and no one can deny its existence. You've brought these men to trial, but they haven't done anything wrong. If Demetrius and his friends have any charges to bring, they should do so through the proper channels. It does no good for the reputation of the goddess or the city if we behave like animals. And in any case, rioting is bad for the tourist trade."

He was certainly a cool customer. His points were valid and his timing was perfect. Without more ado, he declared the meeting closed and ordered the theatre to be emptied. And with that the mob dispersed. The Christians were set free, and the crowd went home.

Divisions

"Whatever's the matter with you?" said Priscilla to Paul one day. "You've been pacing up and down all morning, gnawing your fingers. Don't tell me you're still worried about Corinth." Paul managed a smile. "Priscilla, sometimes you see straight through me. Yes, I'm worried about Corinth. I keep wondering how they're getting on."

Priscilla took his arm. "The trouble with you is you take on to much. You don't really trust God to look after His people do you?"

"Of course I trust God," said Paul, "but I still can't help thinking about them."

"Look here," said Priscilla, "there are plenty of people to share the load. There's that clever man Apollos, for a start. He has a clear mind and he's an excellent speaker. Then there's Titus. You can always rely on him to do a job. And Timothy. I know he's shy, but he can take a letter, and he's been with you long enough to know what it's all about."

It was quite true. There was no point in Paul having a nervous breakdown. He couldn't be everywhere at once, and that was that. So he took to writing letters. Whenever a boat was leaving for Galatia or Corinth or Philippi, Paul would try to send a message. And because no one could make out his writing, he often asked Timothy to put it down for him. That way Timothy learned a lot.

One day, Timothy returned from a trip to Corinth with a rather sombre expression on his face. "The church is having a bad time", he said. "They seem to be splitting into different groups."

"What do you mean, groups?" said Paul.

"Well," said Timothy, "they had some visitors from Jerusalem who claimed to be the original Jesus Movement. They called themselves the Peter Party. Some of the Christians joined them, to be on the safe side. Then Apollos made a very persuasive speech, and some of the others said, 'He's the man for us!' And that left a few who said, 'We're not sure about all these different views, but we stick to Paul. We'll wait until he comes back.' "

"My word," said Paul, "they are getting themselves in a tangle. What with Peter and Apollos and Paul, it seems Jesus hardly gets a mention these days!"

A Stiff Letter

Paul decided to write to the Christians at Corinth. At first he had wanted to pay them a visit, but Aquila advised against it. "Let Titus go," he said, "he's a steady chap, and he'll have much more patience with them than you." So Paul dictated, and Timothy wrote, and Titus delivered the letter.

"From Paul to the Corinthians –
Grace be with you, and peace from God our Father, and from the Lord Jesus Christ.

I beg you to think again about all these divisions. You shouldn't call yourselves after any human leader, however clever or devout he may be. You all belong to the same group, and that group is the Body of Christ. And don't let anyone tell you you're second-rate Christians because you're not Jews, or you don't have one of the spiritual gifts. We don't become Christians to get spiritual gifts. We become

Christians to belong to Jesus Christ. And at the end of the day, what counts is love. You can have every spiritual gift in the book – power to preach, power to heal, power to prophesy – but if you don't have love, you're just a big mouth. So try to love each other. Treat each other as Jesus treats you. Then you won't go far wrong."

Timothy finished the letter and read it through. "That will do", said Paul. "Before I go to bed, I want to finish off that letter to the Galatians. But don't you stay up. I'll write it myself." He picked up the pen and dipped it in the inkwell.

"See what big letters I make as I write to you now with my own hand!" he put, and smiled. Then his face became very stern. He went on, "Don't believe any one who says you can only get right with God by becoming Jews, keeping the Law, not eating pork, not working on the Sabbath, and so on. The Jewish Law never saved anyone. I should know – I lived by it for most of my life. But now I firmly believe that we are put right with God through the death of Jesus on the cross. And if you want anything to boast about, then boast about that! I used to boast about being the perfect Jew. But not any more. There's only one boast in my life now. The boast the Jesus died for me.

"May the Grace of our Lord Jesus Christ be with you all, Amen."

The Collection

Paul was thinking of Jerusalem. How lovely to see the city once more, and take news of the Christians in Europe and Asia. He knew the Jerusalem church had fallen on hard times. He wished that somehow he could help . . .

And then he had an idea. He would start a collection. He would visit all the places where the Christian church was growing, and ask them for a gift for their brothers and sisters in Jerusalem. Then he would deliver the money himself, taking with him a few Gentile Christians, and hoping to be there by Pentecost.

So he set out. Sometimes he went by boat, but he also travelled many miles on foot. Wherever he went, the Christians received him joyfully. But they were worried that he was going to Jerusalem. On one occasion, a prophet called Agabus took Paul's belt, and tied up his own hands and feet. "The owner of this belt will be tied up by the Jews in Jerusalem, and handed over to the Romans", he warned. "If that's all that happens, I'll have got off lightly", said Paul. "Being tied up for Christ doesn't worry me in the least. Why, I've been ready to die for him these many years."

When his boat docked unexpectedly near Ephesus, Paul asked the Christian leaders to come

and see him. It was a fifty-mile journey, but they responded gladly.

"Listen," said Paul, after they had greeted each other, "I may not come this way again. The Holy Spirit tells me that something terrible is going to happen to me in Jerusalem. But I have to go there all the same. We should always support our brothers in trouble, and there are many sick and poor Christians in Jerusalem who need our money. In any case, if I survive this trip, I want to go to Rome. After all, that's the centre of the world, and the Gospel must be preached there too."

It was a sad farewell. They all knelt to pray together, and then hugged Paul and said goodbye. Many wept openly at the thought of not seeing him again; not in this life, anyway. They crowded onto the pier, and stayed there waving until the little boat was completely out of sight.

Arrest

It was a great day for the Jerusalem church when Paul arrived. James and the others welcomed him warmly and listened carefully to all his news. They were very moved, too, that so many Gentile Christians should send money to help them. But James had a word of warning for Paul.

"My brother," he said, "there are thousands of Jews in this city who believe you are trying to abolish the Law of Moses. They also think you have no time for the Temple. It would do a world of good if you could go to the Temple with four others and spend a special week in prayer. That will show anyone who's interested that you still keep the Jewish customs."

Paul agreed with James's suggestion. But when they got to the Temple he was recognized by someone from Gamaliel's school. Immediately the man raised the alarm. "Help! Saul of Tarsus is back. He's in the Temple! He turns Gentiles away from God and preaches against the Law! Catch him quickly!"

In no time at all, Paul was arrested and dragged out of the Temple. The news of his capture travelled fast, and a large crowd gathered. There was a rush to find suitable stones so that they could put him to death, there and then. In the nick of time, a squad of Roman soldiers arrived on the scene. They forced their way through the mob, and pulled off those who were beating Paul. "Now what's all this?" asked the Commander. There was a hubbub from the crowd. Some shouted one thing and some another. "All right, all right," said the

411

commander. "It serves me right for asking. I'm putting this man under arrest, pending further enquiries. Now move along there. Move!"

But the crowd didn't move. They stayed exactly where they were, seething with anger, and shouting "Kill him! Kill him!" In the end, the soldiers had to carry Paul above their heads. It was touch and go as to whether he'd still be attacked and killed, despite the Roman escort. As a gesture to the people, the Commander ordered him to be trussed up with two heavy chains. At last they reached the safety of the fortress.

"Put him down there", said the Commander. "We'll give the little fellow a going-over. Someone get me an interpreter."

"Excuse me, Sir," said Paul quietly, "perhaps the little fellow might say a word for himself?"

"Good gracious, I didn't realize you spoke Greek", said the Commander. "I thought you were

412

that Egyptian who organized some freedom-fighters years ago."

Paul smiled. "I'm sorry to disappoint you, Commander, but I'm a Jew. And before you start the interrogation, I ought to warn you that I'm also a fully-fledged Roman citizen." He showed the Commander his ring. The Commander studied it closely. "That's genuine all right", he said at last. "You don't see many of them hereabouts. I'm glad you showed me that before we whipped you. I'd have been drummed out of the army."

"My name is Paul", said Paul. "I come from the famous city of Tarsus where my father was on the Council. I didn't have to earn my ring. I'm a citizen by birth." The Commander stared at his prisoner with new respect, and hurriedly unfastened the chains.

★

Meanwhile, some Jews were plotting to kill Paul. About forty of them asked the High Priest to summon Paul for questioning. Their plan was to jump the soldiers as soon as they left the fortress, and assassinate the prisoner on the spot. But Paul's nephew got wind of what was going on, and ran helter-skelter for the fortress. He demanded to see Paul, and told him everything. Then, together, they warned the Commander.

"Well!" said the Commander, drawing himself to his full height. "No one kills any prisoners while I'm around. Tonight we'll transfer Citizen Paul to the castle at Caesarea. We'll take a little contingent of two hundred soldiers, seventy horsemen, and two hundred spearmen. That should prove adequate for the task." He looked at Paul. "I'll get

413

you safely away from this rabble or my name's not
Commander Claudius Lysias!"

"Thank you, Commander Lysias", said Paul,
and gave his nephew a sly wink.

414

The Hearing

Once at Caesarea, Paul was put on trial before Felix, the Roman Governor. The High Priest himself made the effort to attend the hearing. He brought with him the very best lawyer available – a man named Tertullus. Tertullus began as follows:

"Your Excellency, I cannot, must not and will not deny that, thanks entirely to your wise judgement and devotion to duty, we are enjoying a period of peace and positive reform. We welcome this everywhere and at all times, and are deeply

grateful to you." He delivered a low bow. "Honoured Felix, if I am allowed to impose upon your valuable time, it is because you are renowned for your kindness. But I will try to be brief." He sniffed apologetically, and looked as though he was about to mention some unsavoury matter. "Your Excellency, you see before you the erstwhile Saul of Tarsus, now answering to the name of Paul. He has been a nuisance to us for many years, causing riots among Jews all over the world. We caught up with him the other day when he attempted to defile the Temple, and we want to see him put away for a very long time."

But Felix was more than a match for this windbag of a lawyer. When Tertullus paused for breath, the Governor said, "Thank you. Let me assure you that this matter has my full attention. I intend to give a ruling in a few days' time. This court is now adjourned."

The truth was that Felix was quite well informed about the Christian faith. His wife, Drusilla, was a Jewess, and had told him all about it. Now he was pleased to meet Paul for himself, and looked forward to many an interesting discussion. After all, it made a change from the tedious procession of thieves and rebels who normally trailed through his court. One evening, Felix sent for Paul and asked him to say a little more about faith in Jesus Christ. Paul needed no second bidding.

"Your Excellency," he said, "I was brought up to keep the Law of Moses. Indeed, I was a very strict Jew, and liked nothing better than to persecute heretics. But then I met with the Risen Christ. I realized that not all the laws in the world could

bring me to God. In fact, they drove me further and further away from him. So now I throw myself on the mercy of God, asking forgiveness through Jesus. And I believe that one day this Jesus will come to judge us all, whether we are followers of his or not. No one can sit on the fence in this matter.

418

Whether we are tent-makers or governors, we must make up our own minds."

"Er, yes", said Felix. "Quite so. We must have another talk about this some time." He turned to his wife. "And now, dear, it's time to lock Paul back in his cell; and we must get to bed."

419

Agrippa

For two years Paul was held in prison at Caesarea. Felix pretended to be interested in the new faith, but in fact he was hoping for a sizeable bribe to set Paul free. Eventually a new governor, Festus, was appointed and the whole case came up for review.

Festus had hardly moved into Government House when a delegation arrived from Jerusalem. They wanted Paul to be brought before a Jewish court without further ado. But Festus wasn't a man to be rushed. Paul was a Roman citizen, and no Roman should have to run the gauntlet of a Jewish court.

And then, some time later, King Agrippa came to pay his respects to the new governor. He was only King of the Jews, which didn't mean much at that time, but it suited the Romans to let the Jews have their little royalty. It was certainly preferable to the trouble-making ruffians who might otherwise try to seize power. And so, every once in a while, it was good public relations to make a fuss of the Royal Family, give them a guard of honour, let them wave from the balcony, and so on. One evening, when Festus and Agrippa were running out of conversation, the Governor suddenly remembered Paul.

"Your Highness," he said, "you're the very man to guide me in this matter. I can't myself see that Paul has done anything wrong, but then I don't understand all the ins and outs of Jewish custom."

"Well now, let me see", said Agrippa, who had been feeling very important all day. "Let us have Paul brought before us so that we can hear his story."

The following day, King Agrippa and Queen Bernice were ushered into the audience hall with great pomp and ceremony, including about a hundred metres of red carpet and a deafening blast on a trumpet. The military top brass were all in attendance, as were the Mayor and Corporation. When all was ready, Festus gave the order for Paul to be brought in. The Governor spoke:

"King Agrippa, this is the man who has your people screaming with rage. I have already decided to refer his case to Rome. But tell me, what can I say to the Emperor? I can't send him without a proper charge."

Agrippa tried to look learned, and raised his voice to address Paul. "Paul of Tarsus," he said, "the time had come to defend yourself." So Paul began to state his case all over again.

"King Agrippa," he said, "you are a Jew and will readily understand these things. We believe, don't

421

we, that Moses and the Prophets looked forward to the coming of the Messiah?" Agrippa nodded. "Well, it is because of my belief that this Messiah has come that I am on trial before you now."

"You know," said the king, when Paul had

finished speaking, "if it was up to me, I'd give you your freedom this minute."

"And so would I," added Festus, "but you appealed to the Emperor, and to the Emperor you must go!"

423

Shipwreck

It was rather late in the year to be sailing for Rome. Paul said as much to Julius, the officer in charge of him.

"I've been travelling in these parts for twenty-five years", he said. "You simply can't rely on the weather after October." Julius was impressed, and they went to see the captain.

"My friend," said Paul, "we're in for at least a dangerous voyage, and we may even lose the ship. My advice is that we spend the winter on the sheltered side of Crete."

But the captain was a proud man. "I'll do the sailing, if you don't mind, sir", he said. "We set sail

424

tomorrow morning, bright and early." And that
was the end of the discussion.

No sooner had they weighed anchor the
following day, and passed out of sight of land, than a
storm began to blow. A north-easter buffeted the
ship, making it impossible to hold a course. After a
bruising morning, they gave up, dropped the sails,
and battened down the hatches. The vessel started
wallowing so badly that they threw a lot of cargo
and equipment overboard. And then the weather
closed in completely. The light was so bad that it
was impossible to tell the difference between night
and day for nearly two weeks. All that time they ran
downwind under bare poles, with despair in their

hearts. And then Paul took command. He raised his voice above the howling gale.

"Men, you should have listened to me when I said we should stay in Crete, but we won't go into that now. The fact is that we will survive, thanks to the mercy of Almighty God. So take heart! I expect to appear before the Emperor in Rome in the not too distant future, and I don't doubt we shall all be alive to tell the tale."

About midnight, they took soundings and discovered that they were in shallow water. The captain was panic-stricken at the prospect of being driven onto rocks and pounded to pieces. Indeed, some of the sailors tried to escape in the lifeboat, but Paul alerted the soldiers. "If anyone leaves this

ship, we're done for!" he said. He was so well in charge by this time, that the soldiers cut the ropes that held the dinghy and cast it adrift without question.

"Now listen," said Paul to the demoralized captain and his exhausted crew. "You're at the end of your tether and that doesn't surprise me. You've had no food or sleep for fourteen days. But cheer up. In a few hours' time we'll all be warm and dry, though I'm pretty sure we'll lose the ship. Now let's have a prayer and then we'll eat the last of the food. You'll need something inside you if we go for a swim."

Soon afterwards, there was a ghastly shudder and the noise of splintering timber. They had run aground.

Journey's End

In the cold light of dawn they could inspect the damage. The ship was hopelessly stuck on a sandbank. Mighty waves were pounding her stern and she was rapidly breaking up. But nearby was the welcome silhouette of an island, and they could already see a gently sloping beach. "Land ahoy!" cried the sailors, "Land ahoy! We're safe at last!" But while the sailors set about abandoning ship, the soldiers grimly marshalled the prisoners. "We can't have you escaping now, can we?" said a corporal. "So we'll have a little execution ceremony before

428

we leave." Julius was horrified at the thought of Paul being put to death, and he quickly intervened. "There's no time for that now," he said briskly, "I want all able-bodied men overboard and swimming ashore by the time I count three. The rest can hang on to pieces of wreckage."

So it was that everyone came safely to dry land. By great good fortune they had been shipwrecked on the island of Malta. The locals were very friendly, and soon built a big fire to warm them up. They were startled to see a snake appear from the firewood and fasten itself round Paul's hand. Of course, he quickly shook it off, but they still expected to see him drop dead. However, they waited a very long time, and nothing happened. They decided he must be a god!

429

The chief official on Malta was a man named Publius. He put up everyone in his house for three days while they recovered from the effects of their adventure. Paul was able to heal Publius' father of a stomach upset, and that led to a constant procession of people with aches and pains coming to the door. When, three months later, the weather was safe enough for sailing, the islanders showered them with gifts and provided all the food they would need.

A few weeks later the ship arrived at the Italian port of Puteoli, and Paul was delighted to discover a group of Christians there. He stayed with them for a week before undertaking the final part of his journey to Rome. As the days went by, he wondered what awaited him in the Imperial City. It was such a long time since he first decided to go there, and there had been so many setbacks. But through everything – riots, imprisonment, shipwreck and snake-bite – God had kept him safe.

To his great joy, some Christians from Rome travelled out to meet him. They greeted him at the town of Three Inns and kept him company for the rest of the journey. He was to stay under house arrest in Rome until his trial came up. A burly soldier would guard his door, but he would be free to read and write and receive his visitors. In particular, there were many Jews in Rome who wanted to discuss Jesus with him.

Paul brightened visibly. It might be many years before his case was heard; and meanwhile there would be plenty to keep him busy.

The Runaway Slave

At last Paul was in Rome. He had achieved the ambition of a lifetime by bringing the good news of Jesus to the heart of the Empire. He knew that if only he could preach and teach here, the Gospel would be carried to every corner of the world. Of course, he had never expected to be in Rome as a prisoner. But he didn't question the way God had done things. He had long since learned that the wisdom of God is not at all the same as common sense.

One day there was a knock on the door and a white-faced young man came in. He stood on the threshold, trembling.

"Hello there!" said Paul. "What can I do for you?" He looked at his visitor more closely. "Wait a minute. Don't I know you from somewhere?"

"Yes, sir", said the lad. "You saw me with my master when we came to your lectures in Ephesus. His name was Philemon."

431

"That's right!" said Paul. "Gracious me, that seems a long time ago. But I'm afraid I've forgotten your name . . ."

"You never knew it, sir", he replied, "it's Onesimus."

"Onesimus, eh?" said Paul. "Welcome to my little house, Onesimus. But tell me, is your master in Rome?"

"No sir," said Onesimus, "I'm by myself. You see," he stared at the floor, "I ran away."

"Dear me", said Paul. "You know you can be put to death for doing that?"

"Yes, sir," said Onesimus, "and in a way I want to die. I came to Rome in search of freedom, but I've ended up hungry, lonely and tired."

"My poor chap," said Paul, "let me get you something to eat." Soon Onesimus was enjoying a thick slice of bread and a hunk of cheese. He also tried some of Paul's homemade wine. While he ate, they talked.

"Onesimus," said Paul, "let me tell you something. True freedom isn't found by running away. Freedom lies in belonging to God." He waved a hand at his little room. "Look at me, for example", he said. "I can't even leave the house. There's a guard on the door. And I've known much worse things than this. I've spent years of my life in prison, chained to a soldier or to the wall." He smiled. "But you know, in myself, I'm as free as a bird! In myself, I know that God loves me and that His Spirit is with me. I'm quite content wherever I am, and I'm not afraid of anything anyone can do to me."

"I wish I was like that", said Onesimus.

A few days later, Paul wrote a letter:
"Dear Philemon,
How are you, old friend? I hope you don't mind,
but I'm writing to ask a favour.

"I'm sending this letter with Onesimus, your
runaway slave. I came across him in Rome, and he
has become a Christian. May I beg you to take him
back and give him another chance? I know it's
asking a lot. But Jesus helps us cross all barriers –
even those between masters and slaves. And when
you think about it, Onesimus is much more than
your slave now. He's your Christian brother!
With love and prayers,

Paul."

433

The Visions of John

The Book

As years went by, many Christian groups sprang up throughout the Empire. They worshipped God as Father and obeyed Jesus Christ as Lord. They believed that one day Jesus would appear again and rule the world.

But meanwhile, these Christians were often persecuted. The emperor Nero blamed them for the Great Fire of Rome, and put many of them to death. Another Emperor, Domitian, set himself up as God. He ordered his entire Civil Service to call him "Lord", and executed his relatives for not worshipping him! Of course, no Christian could ever pray to a Roman emperor, and so they were hounded to death once again.

435

On the island of Patmos, a Christian leader called
John pondered these events. If God was in control,
why did Christians suffer? If Jesus was Lord, why
did his followers get thrown into prison? And then
he had a vision. Later, he wrote it down:

I saw a door in heaven. An open door. A voice
said to me, "Come inside, and I will show you what
must be." There, on a great white throne, sat God
Himself. He was worshipped day and night by all
His creatures, angels and men. As I looked, I saw
that in His right hand was a Book. A closed Book,

sealed with seven seals. And no one in heaven or earth was fit to open it and discover its secrets.

I wept bitterly because no one was fit to open the Book or look inside it. But someone said to me, "Don't cry. Look!" There, standing in the middle of the throne, was the Lamb of God. Everyone in heaven and on earth was bowing down to him, loudly singing his praise: "The Lamb who was killed is worthy to receive power, wealth, wisdom, and strength, honour, glory, and praise!" And everyone said "Amen!"

437

The Horsemen

As the Lamb of God began to unfasten the Book, four great horsemen galloped out of the pages. First was a white war horse, and his rider carried a bow. He rode like a conquering king, and wore a victor's crown. I thought of mighty armies on the move, of the rise and fall of empires . . .

The second horse was red, and his rider wielded a sword. Their eyes were full of fire and their nostrils flared with rage. I thought of battle and pillage, of blood and gore, and smoking ruins in blackened fields . . .

And then a dark horse. His rider held a pair of scales, as if to measure out the future. As he rode by a harsh voice croaked, "Low wages, high prices, shortage and want!" I thought of hunger and dearth, and food being rationed. A few grains of wheat for a whole day's pay . . .

Finally, a pale and eerie horse. His rider wore a shroud. His name was Death. In his wake crept all the shades of Hell. I shuddered. Whoever we are, Death comes to us all . . .

And then I saw a mighty crowd. It was made up of all those who had died for their faith. They were pleading with God for justice. "How long, O Lord?" they cried. "How long before you stop the world and punish the wicked?"

As their voices faded away, the whole cosmos was plunged into darkness. The sun died. The moon turned blood-red. Stars and comets plummeted through space in endless freefall. Suddenly the earth was ripped apart by a violent earthquake. The sea boiled. Then there was a loud thunderclap – and silence. Complete silence, for about half an hour.

The Dragon

And then a great and mysterious sight appeared in the sky: a most beautiful woman with shining robes and radiant face. On her head was a crown of twelve stars. I thought of God's people. That was how they should be. Gentle, pure and bright. I saw that she was expecting a baby.

But horror! A great red dragon, all heads and horns, rose up from the earth. He lashed at the sky with his tail, and advanced on the woman breathing fire. I knew he wanted to devour her child. Before I could cry out, the baby was born. Instantly, he was snatched away to safety in Heaven. Somehow the woman managed to escape.

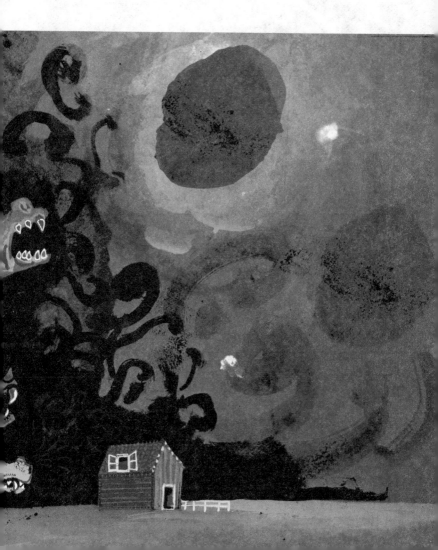

Suddenly the dragon swung round, snarling and snapping. Charging down on him were all the Angels of God, and at their head was Michael. The whole of Heaven was plunged into war as the dragon fought the armies of light. Finally he was overthrown, but not killed. He was turned out of Heaven, along with all his allies, and left to roam the earth. He wrought havoc wherever he went. In

blind rage he chased the woman again. He wanted to take revenge on her for all his loss of power.

But she was given an eagle's wings, and flew to a place of safety. I thought of God's protection, even when Satan does his worst. The Devil has his way in the world. But his power is limited, and his time is short.

The City of God

And then I heard sweet music. A lovely light began to spread across the landscape. The sky arched overhead, a perfect blue. The chatter of children reached me from somewhere nearby.

I found myself walking in the City of God. It wasn't like any city I had ever seen. It wasn't a place

of pride and misery, poverty and greed. It was open
and spacious, with fountains and parks. The
buildings were pleasing to the eye, and lovingly
built. I looked for the sun, but it wasn't shining.
The light, so beautiful and clear, was the presence
of God Himself. I thought of Jerusalem, and looked
for a Temple. But there wasn't a Temple, and there
weren't any churches. Such places were no longer

needed, because God was being worshipped everywhere, all the time.

The gates of the city stood open all day, and there was never any night.

All the people who love God live here. Whatever they have suffered while they lived on earth is made up to them a thousand times over. There is no sickness or disease, no famine or war or death. No one tells lies or picks quarrels, or makes the lives of

others a misery. It's as though the life of Jesus has finally spread to everyone. As though his love and joy and peace were flowing through every heart and flooding every life . . .

And then I heard a voice. The voice of Jesus. Even as the vision of Heaven faded, he said to me, "Tell everyone I am coming. Tell them to hang on, because I am coming soon."

And I said, "Yes, Lord. Hurry up and come!"